BRINGING IN THE SHEAVES

BRINGING IN
THE SHEAVES

Richard Higgs

WITH PHOTOGRAPHS BY THE AUTHOR

COUNCIL OAK BOOKS

Council Oak Publishing Company, Tulsa, OK 74120
©1996 by Richard Higgs. All rights reserved
Book and cover design by Carol Stanton

First Edition
00 99 98 97 96   5 4 3 2 I

ISBN I-57I78-026-2

Library of Congress Cataloging-in-Publication Data

Higgs, Richard, I952–
    Bringing in the sheaves / Richard Higgs: with photographs by the
author.—Ist ed.
      p.   cm
    Includes bibliographical references (p.   ).
    ISBN 0-93303I-98-x (cloth). — ISBN I-57I78-026-2 (paper)
    I. Wheat—Harvesting—Great Plains   2.Wheat—Great Plains.
    3. Higgs, Richard, I952—Journeys—Great Plains.   4. Great Plains—
Social life and customs.   I. Title.
    SBI9I.W5H48 I996
    9I7.80433—dc20

                                    96-I9478
                                    CIP

For Debbie, Jared, and Jennifer

$\mathcal{C}$ o n t e n t s

$\mathcal{P}_{r\ e\ f\ a\ c\ e}$

Every year on the Great Plains of North America an undertaking of epic proportions takes place. By epic proportions I mean thousands of people traveling a vast distance together over an extended period of time, participating in something of global economic, political, and social importance. That something is the harvesting of our wheat crop.

Men and women have followed and worked the wheat harvest in an unbroken rhythm for about ten thousand years. The sowing and reaping of the first wheat crop was a civilizing act, a turning point in the history of our species.

The idea of sowing and reaping wheat, and all that has derived from that idea, has made wheat a powerful symbol, a universal source for archetypal visions. It was in pursuit of such a vision that I spent several months traveling the Great Plains, helping to bring in the sheaves.

. . .

Virtually all of the harvest work in North America is done by the hundreds of custom harvesters and their crews, who start in Texas and journey north, through Oklahoma, Kansas, Colorado, Nebraska, Wyoming, South Dakota, North Dakota, Montana, and up into the Canadian provinces, cutting wheat as they go. Their pace is decided by the weather and the maturation rate of the wheat. They're welcomed everywhere they go, for with the harvest they bring prosperity to small towns and rural communities all up and down the plains.

Though men and women have harvested wheat since time immemorial, the epic scale at which it's done today is a twentieth- century phenomenon.

The custom harvester is a creature of twentieth-century technology and economics. Before the invention of diesel-powered combines with their ability to cut up to a thirty foot swath through the wheat, and trucks to haul the combines and the grain, and modern roads to get from place to place, the wheat harvest was a relatively local event.

In the spring of 1992, I hired on with Alan Nusser, a custom harvester for thirty-five years, from Alva, Oklahoma. I drove a tractor for him from May to August, 1992. I traveled with the crew from Texas to South Dakota, and they continued into Canada. This book is the story of that experience.

There are a couple of things about the book I should clear up at this point:

One: this is not a scholarly work, for I'm no scholar.

Two: this is not "journalism" as we've come to understand the term—reportage of a dispassionate observer.

If you want to read a scholarly work, try *The Great Plains*, by Walter Prescott Webb. It is a wonderful book, and still, after all these years, the standard by which other scholarly works on the Great Plains are measured.

If journalism is what you want, I suggest Ian Frazier's *Great*

Plains. I recommend it highly to anyone interested in a contemporary look at this region and its citizens.

I believe there's an older, more general definition of the journalist: that is, simply, one who immerses himself in a life and keeps a journal of his experiences and impressions. Sometimes he shares those impressions with the rest of us. Perhaps, by that archaic definition, you could call me a journalist, and this book journalism.

I knew from the start that the only way I could tell this story was from the inside out. I'm too shy to try to interview people, and too lazy to research a scholarly tome, but I can drive a tractor, and I can take notes and pictures. I can tell you what happened to me personally, and if the tale has been worth telling, and I've told it well, you might gain a glimpse of the larger picture.

The main text of this book is simply the tale of what happened to me in my pursuit of a specific, purifying vision. I've broken up this main text with some short, informational sections on relevant subjects of interest: how a combine works; one way to bake bread; a short history of wheat cultivation.

In relating my whereabouts during this odyssey, I've refrained, as far as practical, from using political boundaries. This is because I've read numerous journals of eighteenth- and nineteenth-century travelers of the region, and political boundaries, when they existed, were by and large irrelevant to those travelers and their sense of where they were.

What mattered to them was what was physically there: rivers, hills, prairies, woods, settlements, trails, waterholes. It was the same for us. The wheat country isn't a political terri-tory—it's a physical region, and I hope by charting our course in terms of what was physically there to help you see this region in a new light, in its wholeness.

However, I've tried not to be obsessive about this, and if a passage could be clarified by naming a state, then I did so.

Finally, a word or two about the photographs. I used a Pentax KM 35mm camera, lent to me by my sister-in-law, Anna, because the format offered the portability and flexibili-ty I needed to get quick grab shots without neglecting my job as a tractor driver, and member of a team. My opportunities to take photographs were always subject to the requirements of my employment.

I chose black and white film because I could print it myself, thus retaining control over the image quality. Also, I hoped for a certain timeless quality in these images that I've simply never seen in a color photograph.

> ~ *Richard Higgs*
> *1996*

I'd once stepped lightly along a particular cutting e

then, misstepping, I became a falling man.

Vision from a Diner on Route 66

In the spring of 1991 I found myself frying eggs and other things in my beloved wife's diner on Route 66 in Tulsa for a hungry, raucous crowd.

I was there because I'd once stepped lightly along a particular cutting edge, and then, misstepping, I became a falling man. My wife, Debbie, who was always nearby, threw out a net and caught me. Some days I felt saved, some days I felt captured. Over time, I leaned more and more to the latter.

The life of a short-order cook wasn't a bad life, I told myself, but it wasn't my life. The little diner would fill every day with hungry people leaning over the counter to watch me prepare their food, inches away. My performance was an important part of their meal.

My mind began to wander that spring. The diner was hot, noisy, and crowded, and I began to daydream about wide-open spaces out on the plains north and west of Tulsa.

Amid the hiss, the clatter, and the wisecracks of busy lunch hours I thought absentmindedly about the whisper of the wind through grass. Often, with several tickets hanging and the hungry crowd barely at bay, watching me rummage feverishly for this or that ingredient, I'd find myself thinking unexpectedly about the clear, uncluttered horizon of the prairie, and forget what I was looking for. Or was I remembering?

The smell of frying bacon was thick inside the diner. Outside the fogged windows snow melted into the city's gutters. I stepped outside often to breathe, if not to gasp. I pulled the cold, sharp air through my nostrils, and with it the rich, musky aroma of the sodden earth herself, her vapors released by the melting snow of early spring, before the flowers, wafting in over the city from out there, out there.

I was raised in the country.

My cooking began to suffer. I shuffled around behind the counter in something more and more like a dream state. I completely lost track of the date.

Debbie's mother—everyone calls her Mama—did all the baking: biscuits, cinnamon rolls, muffins, buns, and loaves of whole wheat bread. As I would stumble in to open the diner, Mama would be just bringing the last of the bread out of the ovens. The room would fill with the rich, comforting, yeasty aroma, roiling out of the ovens on currents of rising warm air. Then Mama, after a moment's pleasantry, would shuffle out the door, dusted with flour, spackled with dough. I used to wonder what it was like, working alone in the quiet early hours, kneading the warm dough, and watching it rise while the world slowly grew light.

One morning—it must have been around the spring equinox—as brilliant sunlight streamed in through the diner's east windows and set the diner and its occupants aglow, I sliced into a loaf of warm bread. As my knife sank through the loaf and the moist vapors rose up around me, I could see endless fields of yellow wheat, waving brightly under a hard blue sky, with a few small white clouds up high. It was a specific vision.

From that moment the wheat fields became the dominant motif of my daydreams. Yellow wheat, blue sky, white clouds. It was a purifying vision.

Over the following days and weeks this image preoccupied me more and more. I entered it to escape the greasy smoke and din, and it grew to accommodate me. I could see the generous belly of our country sloping down gently from the Rocky Mountains to the Missouri River in sensual undulations carved slowly by slow-moving rivers—a glittering, golden sea waving under a hard blue sky.

I could sense the clarity of the high, open plains—see it shimmering, hear it ringing, feel it winnowing through my hair— and I wanted to gulp the clarity in and make myself transparent.

I became obsessed. I began to listen to the farm report on the early morning drive to work. On my days off I took long drives in the open country.

One day I realized that I knew, and seemed to have always known, that there are people, harvesters, who follow the ripening wheat northward every year, from the Southern Plains to Canada, in a free-form armada of trucks and combines. They are dusty nomads, bringing in the sheaves of North America, hitched to a natural rhythm that men and women have followed unbroken for the last ten thousand years.

I wanted work among them, to help them get the wheat in from the fields. When I talked about it to people at the diner,

I was surprised at how many people I knew who had either worked the harvest themselves at least once, or had friends and relatives who had. It seems to be a rite of passage for many young men just out of high school or college to work the harvest for one season before moving on to more permanent employment. One customer said it was a "male bonding thing" because all her brothers did it and "they always got real dirty together" and seemed to love it. I liked the sound of that.

March became April became May became June.

One day in early June my friend Mike Flanagan came into the diner for breakfast. While I was cooking his breakfast I told him I wanted to work the wheat harvest. He told me he'd done that for part of one season right after high school and had found it a thoroughly unsatisfying experience. For him it had been three weeks of bad food, cheap motels, and unpleasant company.

"It's not that romantic, Richard, believe me," he warned me, eyeing his breakfast on the grill, which I may have been ignoring.

But I didn't believe him. By that time I'd come to consider the North American wheat harvest as nothing less than a heroic, epic event. Imagine—thousands of people and hundreds of trucks and combines chewing their way northward over the vast face of the Great Plains at a pace decided by the weather and the wheat, to feed a hungry world.

It is a monumental task. In the 1990-91 season, the total USDA production estimate was 74.53 million metric tons for the United States and 32.71 million metric tons for Canada. (WASDE-258- September 12, 1991) This crop was

17

spread over approximately seventy million acres in the U.S. (Agricultural Statistics Board, Crop Production Report , USDA. October 1991) and approximately thirty-five million acres in Canada.

When I told another friend, Jim Williams, that I wanted to work the harvest, he told me his sister and her husband are custom harvesters who have worked the harvest for years. I asked him to call them for me about a job, which he agreed to do.

One of my diner waitresses who once lived in the wheat country of north-central Oklahoma gave me the name and number of a harvester she once knew.

I told Debbie that I wanted to quit the diner and go help with the wheat harvest. The part about quitting the diner met with little resistance. She already had a replacement in mind. My cooking had definitely begun to suffer. The part about "going" to help with the harvest was more difficult, but we'd both been feeling more than a little crowded, having to both work together and live together. She could see that I'd become obsessed.

We discussed the matter of my leaving over a three-day interrupted conversation, stopping in mid-sentence, and picking it up again hours later, filling in the gaps in our busy relationship of marriage, work, and parenting. In the end, she thought I should do it.

I made a flurry of long-distance calls trying to locate the leading edge of the harvest where the jobs would be. By this time, it was early July, which was late in the season. The harvest had already reached the Republican River on the Central Plains. I had to move quickly if I was going to catch up.

By the morning of July fourth, I was packed, loaded, and saying good-bye to my family. I had no firm prospects, despite the efforts of my friends, and I could see that I wasn't likely to get any over the phone. I said good-bye to my wife and children individually and collectively. The pain of separation was tempered by my personal excitement and their vicarious excitement over my impending adventure. Even though I expected to be gone for about two months, there were no tears.

The plains must be their own metaphor.

$\mathcal{C}$hasing the Harvest

It was about noon before I finished a series of last-minute minor details and got out of Tulsa.

I crossed the Arkansas River about ten miles upstream from downtown Tulsa, just above Keystone Dam, under a sky swimming in liquid hot blue. Thunderheads were visible low on the northwestern horizon, my intended direction. Just before the town of Cleveland, I saw a Mississippi Kite soar over the road. I don't often see them that far east.

Tulsa isn't on the Great Plains. Tulsa is in a transitional area of oak-dominant forest, called the crosstimbers, and patches of open prairie. The crosstimbers fans out from the west flank of the Ozark Plateau and tapers out in separate fingers a couple hundred miles southwest, across the Red River.

The name crosstimbers is somewhat mysterious in origin, but Carolyn Thomas Foreman offers a plausible explanation in her 1947 book *Cross Timbers*. She theorizes that the name comes from the fact that the forest's separating fingers cross perpendicular to all the major rivers that flow through it from the west-northwest. This relationship of the forest to the rivers made a convenient set of landmarks for explorers in the region. They could rendezvous on the riverbank a certain number of miles up or downstream from a particular finger of the crosstimbers.

East or south of Tulsa takes you deeper into the cross-timbers and up into the Ozark foothills. North and west, the direction I was traveling, takes you out to the open plains. The landscape opens up gradually; the forest becomes islands in the grass, and the islands of grass in the forest become a sea. About fifteen miles northwest of Pawnee, about seventy-five miles northwest of Tulsa, I emerged from the last patches of crosstimber forest.

There wasn't a significant stand of timber left between me and the Rocky Mountains, except for slender riparian strands.

I crossed the Salt Fork of the Arkansas River a few miles south of Ponca City. Calling this middling tributary to the Arkansas a fork of that great river is an overstatement. The Salt Fork is not much more than a hundred miles long and serves a small watershed. In its favor, though, it has wallowed out a scenic valley in its upper end, and its Great Salt Plains Reservoir downstream from Alva is an important refuge for migrating waterfowl on the central flyway.

The first thing you encounter in Ponca City from the south is the domineering Conoco refinery. I drove past the refinery through an entire neighborhood of modest houses that had been bought up en masse and emptied by Conoco as an out-of-court settlement with the homeowners. Something about contaminated ground water.

I plied my way north to Wellington, skirting thunderstorms, and turned west, penetrating further into the plains with each passing mile. I passed through Medicine Lodge on the banks of Medicine Lodge River, then through Coldwater, and then I found myself at a lonely crossroad. I got out and stretched. The ceaseless wind whooshed through the grass. There was a sign at the crossroad that read:

" <— Freedom | Protection —>"

I headed west toward Protection, and sailed right on through a few miles later, after crossing Cavalry Creek.

I wanted to camp at St. Jacob's Well, an oasis that I know. It was getting late in the day and I rolled across the earth with a growing sense of urgency, as I still had about thirty-five miles to go and I don't like to make camp in the dark.

I pulled into the Nature Conservancy preserve that surrounds St. Jacob's Well about eight that night. The late evening sky was a dome of pristine clarity, fading to yellow in the west. When I got out of the car I looked straight up and I could easily see all the way into outer space. It occurred to me that I'd already traveled farther that day than the distance up and out of our earthly atmosphere.

St. Jacob's Well is an ancient oasis that was given its present name by white travelers across the plains in the nineteenth century. The landscape around there is pure shortgrass prairie. I find it supremely beautiful in its stark, lunar stillness. The earth seems to rest at St. Jacob's Well. Or, as Black Elk, the Sioux holy man, once described the stillness of another spot on the plains, "The earth seemed to be listening very hard for something."

I set up my tent as the sun spread itself on the horizon like butter on a hot biscuit.

In the gathering twilight I walked across the cooling earth to a stock tank beneath a windmill and bathed the dust and sweat off me. A family of deer watched me from a discreet distance. Clean, cool, and naked as the earth around me, I walked back to camp and settled comfortably in my reclining lawn chair next to my little dome tent and waited for the stars to come out. I'd been moving relentlessly all day, but now I absorbed the stillness of this place, beyond Protection, beyond Freedom.

I found my angle of repose and looked around. That typical high grassy plain rises gently from south to north in the form of an interlacing network of low rounded hills, open flats, and cutbanks with pubic thatches of woody vegetation gathered in the folds. The color of the prairie varies widely with the season. At the time, it was composed of muted greens and browns. Wildflowers provided bright points of color.

The dominant geological features of that area are two large sinkholes. The larger one to the west, called Big Basin, is about a mile across, and the one hundredth meridian cuts through it. The smaller one, Little Basin, is about a quarter-mile across. I was camped on its rim. The two are separated by a ridge. They're about 150 feet deep with steep sides. On the floor of Little Basin, nestled in a corner, an oasis lies still, dark, and deep, about thirty feet in diameter, under a canopy of old cottonwoods. About halfway across the sink floor the bison that roam the preserve have created a wallow. Their muted lowing drifted over to me from the floor of Big Basin where they were settling in for the night.

I watched the earth's shadow fill the sinks and smaller depressions to the rims and then spill over the land. It washed over me almost like a breeze, tickling my skin. The stars spread across the sky. I lay there on the crater's rim, silent and still. There was a fragile perfection to the moments gliding by that I dared not disturb. It seemed as if my slightest movement might ripple outward uncontrollably and disturb the perfect ascent of the earth into the night.

The lingering smudge of twilight over the western horizon slowly shut down and it was night. I gazed at the Milky Way in wide-eyed wonder on that moonless fourth of July. I counted shooting stars backwards from one hundred until I fell asleep. Sometime later, I was awakened by the sound of coyotes and moved into the tent.

I awoke the next morning before sunrise and looked outside. The sky was already filled with light. I slipped to the edge of the sink and peered down to the water hole, hoping to catch a glimpse of something wild drinking. No luck. I dressed, got my camera, and took a walk across the floor of the sink to the south rim. I was looking for wagon ruts from the nineteenth century. This place is on a line between old Ft. Dodge in the north, and Ft. Supply in the south. I assume that caravans between the two would have stopped here. In the flat early light, however, nothing was obvious.

Colonel Henry Inman, in his book, *The Old Santa Fe Trail*, tells this tale, as related to him by those who were there:

During the spring and summer of 1868 an alliance of Kiowa, under Satanta, Lone Wolf, and Kicking Bird, and

Arahapos under Little Raven and Yellow Bear, began a campaign of attacks against frontiersmen along the Santa Fe Trail that were "unparalleled in their barbarity." Thus, on September 1, General Alfred Sully, a "noted Indian fighter" who commanded the district of the Upper Arkansas, set out from Ft. Dodge in a "generally southeasterly direction" to subdue them. He led a combined force of five companies of infantry and eight companies of the now infamous Seventh Cavalry.

Inman, a true raconteur, says that General Custer was with the expedition at the head of the Seventh Cavalry, but Custer, in his memoir, *My Life On The Plains*, says he didn't rejoin the Seventh Cavalry until after they'd returned. Custer had been court-martialed and suspended without pay in 1867 for leaving his post at Ft. Harker.

Sully's expedition passed right by St. Jacob's Well, and, in that high and dry country, probably stopped to water up on their way south. They may have even stopped there again a few days later during their headlong retreat back north. After a five-day march south-southeast they'd engaged the enemy near the mouth of Wolf Creek on the Canadian River. Fort Supply was later built on that site. In a running battle of several days, the Indians, whose numbers grew daily, drove them all the way back to Mulberry Creek, twelve miles from Ft. Dodge. The troops held out there, exhausted and nearly out of ammunition, until supplies reached them from the fort. That is where Custer rejoined his Seventh Cavalry, took command, and began to prepare them for a winter campaign.

Sully's foray had failed but Custer succeeded a few weeks

later, in November, when he destroyed Black Kettle's Cheyenne village on the banks of the Washita River. Custer's troops attacked the sleeping village at dawn, killed as many men as possible, and captured or killed all the women and children. They killed all the horses, which sickened the troops. Custer is rumored to have taken one of the young women as a concubine. It's been said she bore him a child.

You can't travel in the plains without thinking about Indians. Their legacy is in the names of places, calling out to us from sign posts and stream beds. Cities: Tulsa, Wichita, Omaha, Sioux Falls, Kansas City, Oklahoma City, Ogallala, and dozens of towns and former towns. Rivers: Arkansas, Cimmaron, Niobrara, Missouri, Washita, Neosho, Kiamichi, Pawnee, and hundreds of creeks, wet and dry. Texas, Oklahoma, Kansas, Nebraska, the Dakotas, Iowa, Missouri. The words are so familiar to us all from birth they're part of our common heritage, but they come from the natives, not from Europe or anywhere else.

Plains Indian languages are still spoken by natives because those tribes were conquered really quite recently. The veneer of white culture, like the topsoil, can be thin in places on the Great Plains.

I hiked southwest of Little Basin about half a mile, to a high point, visible for miles, where a cairn has been erected to mark the water hole. It stands about fifteen feet tall, as I remember it. Someone had hung a wooden sign around the cairn with the words "Living Water" carved into it.

I stood on that promontory surrounded by a rising chorus

of meadowlarks and watched the emerging sun etch the dim, flat landscape into brilliant high relief. Every blade of buffalo grass, every dip and rise in the land, every prairie flower, was powerfully exposed by the raking light. My tent was a small green bubble. I was a small, green-clad speck. Then I saw what I'd been looking for. A set of tracks ambled in over the rolling land from a vaguely northerly direction, and went down to the crater's edge not twenty feet from my tent. I couldn't have seen them up close. I needed the elevation, the distance, and the raking light. I searched for the trail's exit to the south, but never definitely spotted it. I briefly considered trying to photograph the trail, but decided it would be futile, even in that ideal light. I'll just have to remember it.

While I was making my way slowly back to camp along the rim I heard something snort, apparently a few yards behind my right elbow. I looked around and much to my surprise, I saw a pronghorn antelope staring intently at me from nearly a quarter of a mile away. We studied each other for a few minutes and then went on our respective ways. I'd noticed the evening before how well sound carries on the prairie because I could hear the bison from nearly a mile away on the floor of Big Basin, and from even farther away I could clearly hear the occasional sound of a car whishing by on the highway to Dodge City.

I sauntered, strolled, ambled, meandered, and dawdled back to camp. I wasn't eager to climb back in my car, but I was a man on a mission, and the sun was climbing the sky, on a mission of its own. I was already beginning to sweat, and the temperature was rising fast. It was time to get moving. I broke camp beneath the gaze of a curious Swainson's hawk and headed north.

A few miles down the empty road, I passed a coyote loping casually along the roadside.

I met and passed a southbound truck. It was an event that took a full two minutes to complete.

I turned the radio on to a country station, which in that country is a redundant statement.

I pulled into Minneola and, seeing a cafe at the crossroads, realized I was hungry. I stopped, went inside, and sat at the counter. A woman approached me.

"Coffee?" She set a cup of coffee in front of me.

"Yep." It was the first word I'd said in a while. It sounded kind of funny.

"Want some breakfast? How about some ham and eggs?"

"Hmm. Could I see a menu?" I took a sip of coffee. Ahhh.

"Honey, we don't have a menu. We have ham and eggs. Now, do you want some breakfast?"

I was amused.

"Sure. I think I'll have the ham and eggs."

She turned and disappeared into the kitchen.

"Do I get to tell you how I want my eggs?" I called out.

She didn't hear me. She was probably already cooking. I looked around. A man in a cowboy hat and a shirt with snap buttons studied a newspaper in the bright morning sun. He wore glasses and stirred his coffee absentmindedly. Steam from his coffee curled upward in the light.

Time passed.

The woman brought me my ham and eggs. They were over medium.

"How's the wheat harvest coming this year?" I asked.

"The what? Wheat harvest? I don't know, hon, it's all over around here. More coffee?" She was already pouring it.

"Yep."

The man by the window eyed me over the top of his glasses. I ate, paid, and left. After fueling up across the street I got back on the road.

A few minutes later I came into Dodge City and crossed the Arkansas riverbed, dry as buffalo bones. The broiling air in Dodge City was alive with the mingled aromas of tourist lucre and beef on the hoof. I didn't linger.

I headed west out of town. The highway follows the Atchison, Topeka, and Santa Fe rail line, which follows the Old Santa Fe Trail, which follows the Arkansas River. After a few miles I stopped, got out, and hiked a couple hundred yards off the road to view the wagon ruts of the legendary old trail. I was amazed. The Santa Fe Trail was abandoned 120 years ago, yet after all the rain, wind, and time since then, the trace is still clearly visible. It seems like a miracle.

The Santa Fe Trail forked at Ingalls, about thirty miles upriver from Dodge City. The left fork crossed the river and proceeded southwest across the Panhandle country. The right fork continued upriver to Bent's Fort, then south-southwest to Santa Fe.

The town of Ingalls has converted an old train station into

a museum, a sort of town attic, like many small-town muse-
ums, with items donated by families in the community. I
stopped in to learn more about the trail. Surprisingly, the
museum has no reference to the trail, which apparently ran
right down the main street, right outside the museum's front
door. I asked the elderly lady in attendance about the trail, but
she knew nothing.

"All you young people come in here with your maps and
such, you know more about the Trail than I do, even though
I've lived here all my life." She seemed almost as surprised as
I was.

Next, I stopped in Garden City to get some fruit, nuts,
bread, and cheese. Garden City is a surprisingly cosmopolitan
town for its size and location. I saw whites, Hispanics, Native
Americans, and Orientals in the grocery store.

Back on the road, at 12:15 p.m., four hundred and fifty-
one miles from my house, Ernest Tubb and Loretta Lynn
came on the radio and sang "Thanks A Lot," with Pete
Mitchell on guitar. For two minutes I was happy in the most
uncomplicated way.

The temperature was ninety-three degrees Fahrenheit, the
relative humidity, twelve percent—brought to you by Cargill.
The road wind roared into my open car windows. West of
Kendall I spied water in the Arkansas riverbed for the first time
since Dodge City.

Rolling through Syracuse, I saw, much to my surprise, a
diner with the name of MACAW'S 66 CAFE. My wife's diner
in Tulsa was named Route 66. I stopped in for iced tea, pie, air-

conditioning, and answers. I got three out of four.

"How'd you come by the name 66 CAFE? We're nowhere near Route 66," I asked the owner/waitress/cashier. Two men next to me at the counter paused in their desultory conversation.

"It's just always been named that," she said simply, looking away.

I headed due north out of Syracuse on an empty two-lane blacktop as straight and level as . . . as . . . well, really straight and level. I was now well out onto the high plains. The harvesters had been there; wheat stubble was everywhere.

I crossed White Woman Creek.

I saw four deer, including a fawn.

I saw a prairie falcon.

If you want to understand the lay of the land you have to know how the waters flow. The Rocky Mountains east of the continental divide are slowly being dissolved and drained to the Gulf of Mexico by a series of major watersheds that cross the plains on their way to the Mississippi River, or directly to the Gulf Coast. Wild young streams tumble down the east face of the mountains, joining, carving deep canyons in the rocks, and depositing the dissolved rocks at the mountains' feet, forming alluvial sediments that have spread and joined over the surface of the Great Plains. These watersheds each form a main channel, a river, that gains volume and loses speed as it winds across the plains, through its previous leavings. This process has gone on since the mountains first thrust, the rivers leaving new deposits and picking up and moving older ones further down, always down, down to the sea.

The most southern of the plains rivers born in the mountains is the Rio Grande, which empties into the Gulf of Mexico; then the Canadian and the Cimmaron, which drain into the Arkansas, which drains into the Mississippi. Further north is the Platte, which ends in the Missouri, which ends in the Mississippi. Other rivers of the plains include the Pecos, the Colorado, the Red, the North Canadian, the Smoky Hill, the Republican, the Niobrara, and the James. And let's not forget the Brazos, the Trinity, the Washita, the Veridgris, the Neosho, the Marais des Cygnes, and the Red River of the North, which is a U. S. river by birth, but Canadian by inclination.

. . .

Not long after I saw the prairie falcon, I saw a sign with an arrow pointing to the left for Mt. Sunflower, the highest point in Kansas, elevation 4,039 feet. This I had to see. I turned off the paved road, and drove west down a dozen or so dusty miles between unfenced fields of wheat stubble. I saw it from about two miles away, an inconspicuous, slightly elevated hillock. A herd of cattle grazed peacefully over it. As a highest point it was a masterpiece of understatement. I drove up a not-too-well traveled two-track to the, uh, peak and got out to admire the view. I could see a little further from up there, it seemed, than from the other hills around, except for those to my immediate west and beyond. But that was Colorado. For all I know I may have been standing beside the lowest point in that state. At any rate, at the pinnacle of Mt. Sunflower, someone has installed in three sections of split rail fence a bronze plaque that reads:

"ON THIS SITE

IN 1897

NOTHING HAPPENED"

The plaque was decorated with a festive bouquet of prickly pear. Next to the plaque someone had jabbed a thirty-five-foot barkless limb into the ground and impaled a cow skull on its upper end, making that the highest object in Kansas.

I made my way back to pavement and headed to Goodland. Just outside Goodland, I crossed over Interstate 70, which slices mercilessly through the plains to link Denver and Kansas City. The highway forms a startlingly intrusive barrier in a land of simple barbed wire, dry creek beds, and lonely two-lanes, like the one I was traveling, that turtles can safely cross. I parked on the overpass for a minute. I didn't have to worry about blocking traffic. I got out to stretch and looked down at one of the major currents of American commerce. Heavy traffic, smelling of diesel, hurled itself along a conduit built to move people and cargo through the emptiness of the plains as quickly as possible, and with as little access as possible to the landscape.

I guess I'm more of a two-lane kind of guy.

Goodland is an important wheat center during harvest. I was a little late, it seemed. The beehive of activity I'd expected to find at the elevator by the railroad tracks wasn't there.

The temperature, according to the local radio station, was 102 degrees. They also reported 109 over east in Salina. A few afternoon thunderclouds were trying to form, but they weren't very impressive. I drove on to St. Francis, crossed the Republican River, and headed for Julesburg on the South Platte River.

I'd hardly seen a standing wheat field since leaving home.

From Julesburg I headed east alongside the Platte to the town of Ogallala. I began at last to see wheat waving in the hot afternoon breeze. Men and machines were busy mowing it down. I could sense that I was hot on the trail of that simple, purifying vision.

A prairie chicken, or maybe a grouse, flew over the road.

Afternoon was fast becoming evening. I welcomed the relief that promised from the heat, and I began to think about where to camp.

I reached Ogallala, a place I'd been curious about, because I like the name, and because it has a colorful cow town history. The first thing I saw in Ogallala was a long line of trucks and combines outside the Motel 8. Very promising. I drove around town for a while to get my bearings. Every motel parking lot was jammed with wheat-harvesting equipment.

Lake McConaughy, an impoundment on the North Platte River, was indicated on my map a few miles north of town. I decided to camp there and in the morning I would try to hook up with one of the crews in town. I drove out to the lake in heavy holiday traffic through beautiful, rolling wheat land.

The wheat was yellow! The sky was blue! The clouds were white! The combines were hungry.

I crossed the dam and found myself driving along the

southern edge of the famous Sand Hills. Driving between the north lake shore and the dunes was like being at the seacoast. Night was fast approaching. I wasted no time setting up camp in a grassy spot off the beach next to a grove of cottonwood trees. Lake McConaughy has wide, sandy beaches, and cold, clear water, not long out of the mountains. This fourth of July weekend, the water's edge was lined with the tents and RVs of thousands of playful people. Colorful sailboats skidded across the water in the waning light. Fishing boats sat at anchor here and there, and ski boats rushed noisily around.

I padded across the sandy beach, nodding at people, and slipped into the lake for a much-needed bath. It had been a long, hot, grinding day on the road, but swimming around in that cold, clear water for a few minutes loosened me up and revived me. I padded back to my tent and put on some clean clothes. During the day I'd developed a monumental thirst, and it was Friday night in Ogallala, a town once called the "Gomorrah of the cattle trail" by Andy Adams.

Andy Adams was a young cowboy who worked the cattle trails from Texas to points north in the 1870s and 1880s. In 1903 he published *The Log of a Cowboy, a Narrative of the Old Trail Days*. This is a fictional tale, but it draws deeply from his years of personal experience on the trails. It's a tale of the ultimate cattle drive, from the Rio Grande River in southern Texas all the way up to the Blackfoot Indian Agency in Montana Territory, near the Canadian border. The story is a masterpiece of the literature of the plains.

He described Ogallala as a town with no churches, but a

variety of saloons, casinos, and dance halls, including the ubiquitous Dew-Drop-Inn.

About the Ogallala Dew-Drop-Inn, Adams wrote:

"Here might be seen the frailty of women in every grade and condition. From girls in their teens, launching out on a life of shame, to the adventuress who had once had youth and beauty in her favor, but was now discarded and ready for the final dose of opium and the coroner's verdict,— all were there in tinsel and paint, practicing a careless exposure of their charms."

I splashed on a little after-shave, and drove to town.

A few minutes later I was sitting alone at the bar in a crowded downtown saloon, whose name escapes me, surrounded by the vigor of college girls in basically one grade and condition: white teeth, shiny hair, supple skin. In attendance was a like number of boys of a similar age and condition. Tee shirts from a certain well-known university located in Lincoln were popular attire. A good time was being had by all.

I kept my own counsel and grew older with every passing minute of bar-time. I couldn't think of a thing to say to anyone, though I badly wanted to join in their easy laughter and ribald camaraderie. After a couple of beers, I settled up with the bartender, a young, athletic-looking fellow. When he brought me my change, I asked him for directions to the Dew-Drop-Inn. He drew a blank.

I shuffled to the door, a lonesome range rider, shouldering past the young and beautiful. I wandered around town, stopped at a few bars, drove back to my tent, and got a good night's sleep.

Next morning I got up and walked across the sand to a well to wash my face and hands. As I struggled with the pump to keep the water running and wash myself at the same time, I looked up and saw a young woman approaching with a pan in her hand. "I'll help you," she said, and took charge of the pump handle while I washed my face with the clear, cold water. "Thank you," I said, rising up to towel off.

She had blue eyes, white skin, and yellow hair.

I pumped for her while she filled her pan. The water splashed her bare feet. We commented on the weather. She had a northern accent. I watched her walk with unconscious grace back across the sand to her people. She walked slowly, taking care not to spill the full pan.

I took my tent down and went to town to look for work. I spoke to numerous crews, granary workers, and even farm implement dealers, all with no success. Someone gave me the phone number of a temporary employment agency set up by the state during wheat harvest to coordinate the needs of harvesters and people like me.

I called the number from a phone booth. Since it was Saturday, the call was forwarded to the agent's home. His daughter answered, and got her mommy, who gave me the numbers of two different harvesters who'd been looking for help, though the leads were a few days old. I called them both immediately, but they'd both already left Ogallala for parts north. I was stymied. The morning was passing. I drove back out toward the lake, where I'd seen some crews working. On the way out, I came across a man unloading a combine by the side of the road. I stopped, and asked him if they needed any help on his crew.

"I think he said he might," he replied, referring to his boss. He began to examine a large crack in the tubular frame of the flatbed trailer holding the combine.

"How can I get in touch with him?"

"Well, he'll be back here eventually, but I can't say when, exactly. He's gone to find a welder. Since it's Saturday, we don't know if it'll take a while or not."

"Where are you all from?"

"Nevada, Missouri."

"Where are you headin'?"

"North. Above the Missouri River—till this happened."

"You mean you aren't going there now?"

"No. I mean yeah, just not till we get 'er fixed, that's all."

During the next couple of hours I talked to three or four working crews, but had no luck. I'd thought it would be easier. During that time I made a point of driving by the disabled rig several times. I never saw the boss man, and the last time I drove by, the rig was gone.

So I headed north, still chasing the elusive leading edge.

I chose a route that would take me right through the heart of the Sand Hills, a place I'd always wanted to see. It's a strange, beautiful country of open, rolling, treeless dunes, covered with lush prairie grasses. About thirty miles into it, due north of Lake McConaughy, I drove slowly through the town of Arthur. It was a small, shady island in a vast rolling sea.

Comparing the Great Plains to a sea is such a natural,

historic, automatic response when groping for words to describe the plains' visual impact, that the comparison almost seems to have gone beyond cliche, beyond analogy, beyond metaphor, to the simple truth. But in fact, the sea remains an inadequate analogy for this land.

We need words to adequately convey the apparent stillness of this landscape. Looking out across the boundless, rippled surface of the plains from a promontory, you don't see the restless motion of a churning sea, you see a place that appears to be quietly resting. The wind may blow past your ears and wave the grasses around, but the further out from your feet you look, the less apparent this trivial stirring becomes, as it is overwhelmed, absorbed, by the overall stillness stretching out all around you to the horizon. The parallax of motion.

I've searched in vain for alternative imagery, a more apt analogy for the visual impact of the plains. The plains must be their own metaphor.

So, if it's not a small, shady island in a vast, rolling sea, what is the simple truth about the town of Arthur? What are the words? Arthur is a small, isolated shade-tree community in the vast treeless Sand Hills region of the endless, sun-baked Great Plains of North America. Arthur is perfectly beautiful. Hardly a leaf stirred at my passing through, which took but a minute.

Another thirty miles or so deeper into the Sand Hills, I pulled onto the meager shoulder of the two-lane road, got out with my camera, slipped through a barbed wire fence, and started walking west. The dunes had become impressively high. I wanted to get off the road and photograph the view from a high point. After a strenuous, thirty minute hike up and down steep, sandbur-covered slopes, I reached a high point with a panoramic view.

A small lake lay at the foot of the hill. A few cattle grazed around one end of it. Above, in a sky as dynamic as the land was static, a mighty flotilla of puffy clouds was streaming out of the northwest. Their shadows raced across the dimpled land, hugging the terrain. Every second was a different arrangement of light and shadow. I had to consciously stop myself from taking pictures, having only a finite amount of film, confronted with an infinite number of pictures.

I heard the scree of an agitated hawk somewhere above me. I scanned the restless sky, shielding my eyes. He sounded very near, but eluded my sight. Eventually, I spotted him, soaring on an updraft. My presence agitated him. He worked his way over to me on the wind, and dipped down close, checking me out. I took his picture. He was a Swainson's. Once his curiosity was satisfied, he went on his way. On my way back to the car, I flushed a Long-billed Curlew—a first for me—and got a picture of him, too.

Later, I sat on the rear end of my car, picked burrs out of my socks, and thought about how long it had taken me to spot that hawk. It's surprising how easy it is for a man to hide on the open plain, but it's even more surprising how easy it is for a hawk, or for that matter, a jet plane, to hide in the middle of an open sky, with nothing between viewer and viewee except air molecules and pure distance. The sky above the plains reminds us how limited our angle of vision is.

A truck lumbered by pulling a combine, headed north. I'd seen no wheat production, or any other crop except some hay, in the Sand Hills. The land seems to be used for cattle grazing or left alone. I gave the truck a fifteen-minute lead, and followed him north.

The next town I came to was Whitman. I stopped at the Whitman General Store and bought a cup of homemade frozen butter pecan yogurt from Katy, the pretty young proprietress. She was doing some paperwork that gave me the impression that she was home from college. I asked her to stand in the doorway of the store behind the screen, and I took her portrait.

Mullen was my next stop. I gassed up at Paul's gas station. Full service!

"Well!" Paul exclaimed as he came up to the car. I was getting out to refill my canteen. "That's two Okies in a row! Are you travelin' with the folks in the red Prelude?"

"Nope."

"They said they were from Oklahoma City. Where you from?"

"Tulsa."

"Fill 'er up? I been to Tulsa. They got the worst damn freeway system there that I ever saw. No offense."

"That's all right. Yes, fill 'er up. Do you have a faucet where I can fill my canteen?"

"You bet, right over there. We got naturally cold water

around here, and plenty of it. The Ogallala Aquifer. Right below the surface. God, I hate interstates. I say they're just canals. Canals for cars. That's one reason I moved out here. No interstates.

"So you're not traveling with that other couple? Quite a coincidence. They just left not ten minutes ago. Said they were lookin' for the Badlands. I sent them north. It's the best route to the Badlands. Where are you headin'?"

"Lookin' for the wheat harvest. Any suggestions?"

"North. Definitely the best route to the wheat country. And a real pretty drive, too."

"Thanks." I headed north.

After crossing the Middle and North Loup Rivers, I reached the end of the Sand Hills at the banks of the Niobrara River.

The Niobrara is the most beautifully named river I know. The Niobrara. I had traced it with my finger on maps and said the word out loud. What does it mean? It sounds exotic, African somehow. I suppose it is exotic. It depends on your point of view.

Perhaps its entry in, say, the Encyclopædia Mongolia might read:

Niobrara River: A clear, fast-flowing stream rising up out of the Great Plains of North America near the white settlement of Lusk, Wyoming, USA, in the vicinity of Latitude 42 deg. 45 min. N. and Longitude 104 deg. 30 min. W. From its source on the High Plains, the waters of the Niobrara flow east to the great Missouri River 447 miles away. The town of Niobrara, named for the river, is situated on a high hill overlooking the confluence of the Niobrara and the Missouri. The Niobrara defines the northern edge of the Sand Hills, an extensive area of grass-covered dunes, in the middle of the vast Great Plains, or Great American Desert, of North America. The Niobrara flows through the old hunting grounds of the Sioux, a Native American people, and not far north of the Niobrara are the reservations of the remaining Sioux Tribes, adjacent to an inhospitable area known as "The Badlands."

The name Niobrara is from the aboriginal Sioux language and means, simply, "running water." It is so named, presumably, because its flow is unusually full, clear, and consistent for a stream of that semi-arid region of the North American continent. The Niobrara drains a rather small watershed (12,000 sq. mi.) for a river of such length, making its consistently strong flow even more unusual. The Ogallala Aquifer, an extensive aquifer which underlies much of the Great Plains, approaches the surface in the vicinity of the Niobrara. The Niobrara River has a small number of tributaries and only a few small, scattered human settlements along its banks, so its waters are also rather clean.

I loved the Niobrara, I confess, before I'd even seen it. I descended into its deep valley and bathed in its waters. Now I love it more than ever.

When I reached the Niobrara it was late afternoon, and I was thinking about supper and shelter for the night. After bathing in the river, I drove out of the canyon up onto a flat tableland. The flora suddenly, unexpectedly, included pine trees. Not far from the Niobrara is the town of Valentine.

On one side of Valentine is the Rosebud Indian Reservation, and on the other, across the Niobrara, is a herd of bison in a wildlife preserve.

I drove through town, looking it over, while I pondered where to camp.

Valentine is a classic American small town of the plains, with a wide main street lined with two- and three-story brick buildings built mostly in the early twentieth century. You know when they were built because the men who built them proudly inscribed the year in stone. The north end of the main street ends in a shady canyon. The canyon is the city park. I drove slowly through it. A quiet stream ambles through it under a high canopy of cottonwoods. Camping is not only permitted, it's encouraged along the stream bank. A random scattering of tents lined the bank. There is no fee or registration required.

A family was having a picnic by the stream. Elsewhere, another family was playing horseshoes. Two young couples were playing volleyball.

I picked a spot to pitch my tent, but first I wanted to eat, so I drove back down Main Street to the Koffee Pot Cafe. The Koffee Pot is a spotless, almost obsessively clean place with antique woodwork on the counter and bar-back, and a freshly painted pressed tin ceiling. It was attended by two young women.

Three of the town elders sat together at one end of the counter. Three pairs of suspenders stretched over unanimously round bellies and hooked into three pairs of Sans-a-Belt slacks.

I sat down at the counter a few feet away, and tried vainly to eavesdrop as one of the old men murmured an off-color joke intended to embarrass the waitress. I only caught the punch line which was recited louder than the rest of the story: "What's so exciting about that? I don't know, but she squeezed about a quart of water out of it!" The waitress very kindly pretended to be abashed as a collective chuckle rippled through the sagging jaws of the old men.

"God! You guys!" she said and pulled away from them to wait on me. While she greeted me and we negotiated my meal, the old man repeated his joke for the benefit of the man next to him who was wearing an apparently defective hearing aid. Again, to my disappointment, I heard only the mysterious punch line.

I ordered pork chops, hash browns, tossed salad with ranch, a roll, and black coffee. When she brought my coffee, I asked the waitress where the wheat country was north of Valentine.

"I really don't know," she smiled, "I just moved up here myself, from Omaha. I do know we've had a steady stream of combines rolling through here all day, though. One of them knocked the green light off our red light."

My supper arrived in good time and I thoroughly enjoyed it. Afterwards, I lingered over a second cup of coffee and tried to eavesdrop on the three old men, but all I ever heard was an occasional enigmatic punch line and a ripple of laughter. Then the repeat.

"So," I asked the waitress as she passed by, "what's happening in Valentine on Saturday night?"

"Sweetheart Gardens," she replied over her shoulder. "That's where everybody goes."

I found a pay phone, called home, and spent a few minutes being pleasantly passed around among my wife, son, and daughter. I told them to look for Valentine on the map.

I went to the park and pitched my tent as afternoon dissolved into evening. Then I set out for the Sweetheart Gardens to observe the locals at play. On the way I noticed an unassuming place called the Corner Bar. "LIVE MUSIC TONITE." I walked in. It was so dark and smoky that I couldn't see at first. My eyes stung. My sense of smell took over and I picked up a complex mixture of beer, piss, tobacco, hot vacuum tubes, sweat, perfume, deodorizer, disinfectant, halitosis, nacho cheese chips, vinegar, popcorn, talcum powder, motor oil, and, possibly, blood.

In time I could see that the barstools were all occupied, so I took a seat in an empty booth in a dark corner. The crowd was mostly Native American. While I waited for the waitress to spot me I watched the band tune up. The band was two middle-aged Sioux named Cecil and Ed. From the looks of their clothes I guessed that they'd had to work on their car on the way to the gig. Their equipment consisted of two guitars, two mikes, a drum machine, one amp, and a mixer. Everyone who walked past them on the way to the restroom paused to offer them a word of advice on tuning.

Eventually they began to play. Cecil was the leader, and

he got a ragged-edged, feedback-tinged sound from his guitar, the likes of which I hadn't heard since Neil Young played with Crazy Horse. Seriously. Cecil had gotten his licks down pat a long time ago and never forgot them. His style and choice of songs made me nostalgic. He was, or is, also a great blues singer, singing songs the rest of us have more or less forgotten about, from a dirty, well-thumbed spiral notebook. His voice was full of surprises, due partly to his imaginative phrasing, partly to his Sioux accent, and partly to his missing teeth. He may have been hampered by a lack of range, but he worked around it. Ed did his best to keep up and even provided occasional harmony.

Near the end of "Mountain of Love" the amplifier developed an annoying buzz. When the song was over, Cecil flipped a switch and the buzz went away. Then he launched into an inspired version of "Midnight Special." Cecil played and sang with fire, passion, and real pain, as if he'd written the song himself from bitter personal experience.

He played a solo on his old, tube-amplified Fender that left me smiling in the dark with grim satisfaction.

Ed just smiled and played along, happy as a clam, but ever since Cecil had flipped that switch, not a sound had come out of Ed's guitar. Neither Ed, Cecil, nor anyone else in the room besides me seemed to notice.

When they finished the song I heard the sound of one man clapping. It was me.

They played for a while longer and went on break. That's when I left, after first watching Ed use his status as a member of the band to cajole a beer out of the bartender. It worked, but I'd say just barely.

I stepped outside, blinking in the fresh air and clear evening light. My smoke-stung eyes recovered as I walked down the sidewalk to Sweetheart Gardens.

Sweetheart Gardens is a beer garden in a courtyard annexed to a large restaurant in a big building on Main Street. The courtyard is surrounded by a high wooden fence. In the middle of the courtyard is a sort of elongated gazebo, from which bartenders dispense beer on summer Saturday nights. A flagpole rises up out of the courtyard, its base surrounded by flowers, and by spotlights shining up on the flag. There are numerous picnic tables. One end of the courtyard is roofed over, with a dance floor and bandstand underneath.

When I arrived, it looked like the entire white community had turned out, and was enjoying itself immensely.

I ordered a beer and looked around. It couldn't have been more different from the Corner Bar.

I saw a bespectacled grandfather dancing with a little girl, who was riding on his shoes. I saw a young married couple sharing a beer, murmuring, the breeze mixing their hair. A half-dozen teenage girls sat at a table giggling, with a group of boys hovering over them. Two preteen girls were teaching each other dance steps. Two little boys secretly traded hits from neighboring tables while their families visited with each other over beers and french fries. The men mostly dressed in the plainsman tradition: cowboy hat or Cargill cap, starched western shirt, blue jeans, boots, and big belt buckles. The women liked tight Guess jeans, and silk-like blouses. Virtually everyone was beautiful, and as blonde as Custer's grandchildren.

There was such an air of law-abiding, cavity-fighting, family- oriented wholesomeness that I began to get a little ecstatic by the end of my second beer.

The band was a big contributor to my burgeoning bliss. Four clean-cut young guys, outfitted in the grand Buddy Holly tradition of two guitars, bass, and drums, played through a litany of popular American music from the last thirty-five years or so. They sang the old Everly Brothers song, "Devoted To You," with a sweet breeziness that perfectly matched the July night. Then they chugged their way through a tough, southern style "Gimme Three Steps." Then the tender "Blame It On Midnight." Naturally, they did a couple of old Buddy Holly numbers; one rocker, one ballad.

The young girls danced, the children played, the lovers kissed. The old folks smiled, the bartenders poured, and my gaze drifted up to the stars swimming in the summer night sky. A warm southern breeze tousled all our hair, and billowed the spotlit American flag above us.

The band began to sing that old Temptations tune, "My Girl," slowly, very slowly, and sweetly, like a hymn. We all knew the words, and some of us began to sing along quietly. We were the safest people on earth, surrounded by our own kind, surrounded by our fields, deep in the very heart of conquered America, singing a song that we all knew. What was left out here that could possibly harm us?

It grew late. The crowd began to thin. The Indians were bedding down on the reservation just north of town, and the bison had been sleeping for hours on their reservation just east of town. Perhaps they dreamed of each other, separated by the Niobrara, and by us. We were getting a little sleepy, too.

Eventually, I found my car, parked outside the Corner Bar, and drove it carefully back to my tent, singing to myself, "What can make me feel this way?" I remembered a poem, or part of one, by Badger Clark, the noted cowboy poet:

The trail's a lane, the trail's a lane.

Dead is the branding fire.

The prairies wild are tame and mild,

All close corralled with wire.

It rained during the night.

The next morning, the seventh of July, I stayed in bed longer than usual for some reason, and didn't get packed and out of town until 9:15.

Black Elk called July "the Moon of Red Cherries."

While I was taking down my tent I noticed that a neighboring camper, who was doing the same, had South Dakota license plates. I asked her where the wheat country was. She told me to try Winner, northeast of Valentine. "Lots of wheat around there."

So, I drove north to Mission, in the Rosebud Reservation, and turned east to Winner. If I didn't find a harvest crew to hire me in Winner, I would have to give up and head south. Although I'd already missed the point, which had been to work the harvest from the southern plains to the northern plains, I wanted to try this one last place.

Outside Mission, I crossed back east of the one hundredth meridian for the first time since St. Jacob's Well.

On the way to Winner I drove through a prairie dog town, and I saw two wild turkeys feeding in the ditch.

I stopped at Carter. Only two things keep Carter from being a ghost town: a thriving church, and the near-absence of standing buildings on its former main street. Of the two long-abandoned buildings left standing, one is a picturesque old hotel. I got out of my car to photograph it, under a mackerel sky. A cool, stiff north wind blew through the grass.

I arrived at Winner, the "pheasant capital of the world," about eleven. Winner, population about four thousand, except during pheasant season, has two walk-in and two drive-in theaters and two video rental stores. I drove around town, looking things over, checking the motel parking lots for signs of harvesters. I didn't see much.

I drove out north of town a few miles and climbed a granite hill and took some photos of the countryside. On the way up I flushed a pheasant. The wind was strong out of the northwest. High thin clouds flew over in bands. The view was impressive. Wheat farms spread out below me in all directions. The farm houses were tucked into thick, evergreen shelter belts facing the north and west. The harvest appeared to be about seventy-five percent in. I could see only one working crew. The grass on the hillside was unusually thick, long, and varied. It was difficult to wade through.

This country is beautiful and fertile in the spring and summer, but it must be bleak, barren, and dangerous in the winter.

I went back to town and found a crew of harvesters in a parking lot, gathered around a truck. A man was under the truck replacing the drive shaft.

Everyone turned to watch as I parked and got out of the car. I walked up to them and asked them if they needed a good hand.

The two men in charge, Randy Jungwirth, and Wayne Frericks, exchanged glances, and Randy said, "No, not really. We could have used one a week ago."

We talked for a couple of minutes before I left.

I drove away realizing that I'd missed the wheat harvest of 1991.

I stopped in the Winner Museum east of town. Winner was made possible by the Dawes Act of 1887, as must have been a lot of towns on the plains. The Dawes Act broke up the reservations into individual allotments of 160 acres per Indian family, so they could become farmers. All reservation lands left over after the allotments were made available for sale to white settlers and developers.

The Dawes Act was a death blow for the traditional way of life of the Plains tribes though it was seen by its backers as the only solution to the dilemma of ever-more whites encroaching upon an ever-smaller portion of land nominally reserved for natives. They felt that reserving large, increasingly coveted, tracts of land for the Indians to roam freely as they always had would have the tragic result of ultimately exterminating them through an unending series of conflicts with white settlers. They were probably right.

They didn't see, maybe they couldn't have seen, the tragic results: not extermination, but displacement, fraud, poverty, alcoholism, and depression, would accompany the ending of a way of life.

Two speculators, the Jackson Brothers, developed the Winner townsite not long after the turn of the century. They convinced the Chicago, Milwaukee, and St. Paul railroad to terminate a spur there from the town of Dallas. Dallas was a railhead about twenty miles southeast of the Winner townsite.

Other speculators had developed a similar townsite two and a half miles south, called Lamro. Apparently quite a fight ensued between the two hopeful communities for the attentions of the railroad; everyone knew that it was a lifeline that would only be thrown to one. Finally, after a rancorous, violent debate, the railroad chose the Jackson Brothers' site. The Jacksons named the town Winner to commemorate their victory. The first thing the citizens of the doomed town of Lamro did after their defeat was to move their homes and businesses—lock, stock, and barrel—to Winner. The only thing left of Lamro today is the bank vault, sitting in a field out on someone's farm. Winner incorporated in 1907.

Twelve pheasants were released in the area in 1911. They have proliferated.

The railroad, so critical to the birth of Winner, has since been taken out. You can still see where it came through town by the arrangements of the buildings along its right-of-way, as well as by its trace.

In downtown Winner, the Peacock Bar, among others, services the pheasant hunters who flock here every winter. I stopped in for a beer.

Four men in various stages of intoxication carried on a sparring conversation that staggered between the topics of fighting and fornicating so unconsciously, and so frequently, that it was as if they were the same topic. They made several tentative efforts to include me in the conversation, but I wanted no part of it.

I piddled the rest of the day, driving around, taking pictures. I spent an hour a couple of miles northwest of town watching a family of four wild turkeys feeding in a ditch as the sun slipped away. I had a leisurely supper in a busy cafe in an old bank building.

After supper I drove out to a field of wheat stubble, and set up my tent in the tall grass by the edge of it. I settled in for the evening and listened to the pheasants clucking and chirping all around me. I'd pitched my tent right over the tall, thick grass and, pressed down, it made a wonderful mattress. Soon, I was asleep. I slept better that night than I had in a long, long time.

I woke up well rested the next morning at about six, after a chilly night. The pheasants were stirring, and the sun arose not long after me with a desperate blaze of color. Then it was lost for the day, above the thickening clouds. I heard low, mumbling thunder in the northwest as I packed my tent.

By seven I was sitting in Sargent's Cafe in Winner, sipping on a cup of hot coffee. Rain began to smear the plate glass and the cafe filled with customers.

I hung around the area until ten o'clock, as the world turned wetter. Then I pointed my car southeast and headed toward home.

A harvest river, carrying this overabundance of

to the sea, and out to the hungry world.

$\mathcal{B}$ a c k   t o   T u l s a

For the first fifty miles or so the road followed the abandoned railroad right-of-way through wheat and hay country. The leading edge of the rain was traveling the same direction as me. We played cat and mouse.

I drove the divide between the Ponca and the Niobrara, through the town of Butte. Just past Butte, a concerned citizen with a gift for succinctness had posted a series of hand-painted signs along the roadside. They read as follows: "CONCERNS"; "AQUIFIER"; "RAINFALL"; "WATER TABLE"; "SPRINGS"; "WETLANDS." I stopped to photograph them, and heard coyotes yapping, though it was midday.

Eventually I came to the Niobrara River, and followed that stream to its mouth on the Missouri, where Lewis and Clark, on their way upriver, had encountered the Ponca Indians. A National Park has been installed on the high ground between the two rivers.

I descended into the valley of the confluence, and crossed the Niobrara River. The town of Niobrara was on the other side atop a high hill. I'd looked forward to seeing it, but was truly disappointed when I did. Niobrara, in its present incarnation, is a Corps of Engineers town. The original townsite in the valley was abandoned for the Lewis and Clark lake project on the Missouri River and the Corps prepared this new site for the town. If you've ever seen a Corps of Engineers town, you will understand my disappointment. The Corps builds a great dam, but they have no idea how to build a town. Corps towns have no souls, no centers, no histories. They're indistinguishable from each other.

It's not the Corps of Engineers' job to provide souls, or histories, to replace the ones they bulldoze and inundate. I know that's up to the people who move into the high-ground sites the Corps prepares for them.

But the physical plan of a town is obviously central to its ability to grow into something more than a collection of buildings, and the Corps seems to give this little, if any, thought.

These towns are all relatively new, so it's still possible that some of them will prosper, their histories will accrete in individual ways and they will form individual identities. As for now, though, they're all similarly bland and unpleasant to look upon.

Sioux City was my next destination, and I arrived in a heavy rain just in time for rush hour. I spent a confusing, frustrating hour trying to find a way down to the riverbank. I'd imagined Sioux City as the northernmost port on the Missouri River to serve the wheat barges that carry the wheat downstream to New Orleans and the world. I'd pictured trucks and barges lined up at a bustling river terminal. It may be true; I don't know. Getting to the riverfront was more than I was able to manage. I gave up and headed downstream toward Omaha.

On the way to Omaha I passed through the Omaha and Winnebago Indian Reservations in lush corn country. The rain stopped for a while.

In the town of Ft. Calhoun, I walked around the reconstructed site of old Ft. Atkinson on the river bluffs. From there I could hear outbursts of cheering from across town. I investigated, and found a girls' state finals softball playoff in progress in a muddy new playing field.

A few miles later I made Omaha. Omaha is much more of a city than I'd expected it to be. It seems to me to be America's westernmost Eastern city. It's a city of neighborhoods. I checked into a motel, and went sightseeing. Getting to the riverfront in Omaha was nearly as difficult as it had been in Sioux City, and when I did, the river of commerce I'd expected, choked with wheat barges being loaded from granaries by hearty dock workers, wasn't there.

Where was our nation's elusive wheat crop?

. . .

Downtown Omaha has a "bricktown" district. There's a trend among cities out here in the interior, of designating old decaying brick warehouse districts for development into trendy restaurant/bars, nightclubs, gift shoppes, boutiques, and the like. These "bricktown" districts are all variations on the same theme, in Dallas, Memphis, Oklahoma City, Kansas City, St. Louis, Omaha, and probably others.

I had a late supper and drove back to the motel through a melodramatic, Wagnerian storm.

I slept poorly the sleep of motels until deep into mid-morning, and woke up drowsy and thickheaded.

After getting up and around and having coffee, I went to the Union Pacific Railroad Museum at that company's building in downtown Omaha and spent a fascinating two hours looking over the exhibits. Among many other things, they have, in a glass case, the scalp of a railroad worker who was attacked by Indians, survived, and got his scalp back. He'd intended to have it sewn back on, but was never able to get it done.

I left Omaha for Kansas City. When I crossed the Platte River south of Omaha, it was in a near flood stage. The roiling water was covered with cottonwood tufts, swirling downstream. The town of Plattsmouth has a self-descriptive name and some classic late-nineteenth-century American architecture in its bustling downtown. I crossed a toll bridge there to the east side of the Missouri River.

I kept an eye out for wheat barges on the river as I drove south in its flood plain, parallel to the Burlington Northern's railroad tracks. Numerous grain trucks passed me headed north.

I crossed Squaw Creek and Nodaway River, listening to country music on the radio.

I drove around in the historic town of St. Joseph.

In a tourist visitor center, a worker told me over a cup of coffee that the Missouri River had been in a "drought condition" for the last five years, and barge traffic had been severely curtailed.

Oh. But what about my expectations? I expected a harvest river, carrying the concentrated, gleaming wealth of our nation's interior; a river choked with the season's commerce, teeming with barges overflowing, and followed by clouds of gulls, white against the deep blue sky; a harvest river, carrying this overabundance of ours down to the sea, and out to the hungry world.

. . .

I pulled into Kansas City about 7:00 p.m, and spent an hour or so working my way down to the riverfront. I'd spotted a huge grain terminal by the bank of the Kansas River, near its confluence with the Missouri. When I finally got to it, I found two trucks lined up to unload wheat. A rusty pipe crossed over the street to a barge pier, where two barges full of wheat were moored. Fat, scruffy pigeons crowded the surly gray sky. I took a picture.

I called my wife, and then had supper in a German restaurant in the Plaza. On the table was a table tent advertising a German beer made from wheat. I ordered a bottle but they didn't have any, had never had any, and the waitress couldn't explain why they advertised it on a table tent. She removed the table tent.

The air that evening in Kansas City was oppressively humid. The world and its denizens grew torpid, as though time itself were having to struggle against that syrupy air.

A thin, oily film formed on sidewalks, plate glass, table-tops, and faces. Heavy storms were being reported throughout the area.

Despite everything, I thought, we're all still subject to the weather. As my uncle Bud once said, "They can put a man on the moon, but not if it's raining that day in Florida."

The skies above the plains are a battleground. Cold, dry air from Canada and warm, moist air from the Gulf of Mexico ebb and flow over the unresisting plains. Where the two air masses meet there is violence.

There's an amazing variety of weather on the plains. I've lived in Tulsa, at the edge of the plains, for twelve years. During that time I've seen temperatures as high as 115° and as low as -15°. I've seen droughts that turned all our lawns brown and killed our gardens. I've been in floods, one of which had my wife floating on her sofa down the street past her car top.

The plains are justly famous for their tornadoes. I've been close enough to one to hear its roar, though I've yet to actually see one. I'm sure I will. I've seen the devastation they leave in their wake. When a tornado rips across the countryside it causes panic, chaos, and awe. Sirens go off. People stand on their porches with camcorders aimed at the dark, churning sky. Shivering trees show the undersides of their leaves. Children hunker down in the hallways at school, or hide under their mothers at home. People fling themselves from their cars into muddy ditches and cling to roots until it's over. Meanwhile volunteers place themselves in the tornado's path to look upon it and tell us what they see, live on the radio, their voices breathless and choked with excitement, distorted from yelling into the mike:

"Looks like a wall cloud, Chip, a wall cloud may have dropped—yes! A wall cloud has definitely dropped down right in front of me, about a quarter of a mile away, Chip, down from the bottom of the main cloud, rotating, trailing ugly streamers, the lightning is ceaseless. The funnel, if it's in there, could drop down out of that wall cloud any second! It's an awesome sight, Chip! The rain outside my windshield is torrential! My car is being, being rocked back and forth! Are you getting a funnel on radar? The rain has stopped now, parting like a, like a veil ... WAIT! THERE IT IS! TORNADO! TORNADO! SEEK SHELTER! IT'S HEAD, ER, TIP IS EMERGING NOW WITH TERRIBLE SLOWNESS OUT OF ITS, OUT OF ITS, ITS SHEATH, ITS CONTAINMENT, AS IF IT'S BURST THROUGH THE VERY SEAMS OF THE SKY, CHIP! ...(MUCH STATIC HERE)...STILL IT COMES, MESMERIZING IN ITS INTENSITY. IT'S ALMOST FULLY EXTENDED NOW, SO PALE, SO ALMOST RIGID LOOKING AS IT SEEMS TO BE SEEK-ING OUT THE EARTH, LOOKING FOR A WEAKNESS, AN ENTRY, SOMETHING! I'M GETTING OUT OF HERE, CHIP! REPORTING LIVE, THIS IS SHERRY BERRYHILL FOR KVOK!"

Survivors of a tornado remember the day the rest of their lives. They tell the tale to their grandchildren years later.

Weathermen, those mild-mannered, bespectacled gentle-men, become our heroes during tornadoes, the men we turn to to save us from this awful thing, to lead us to safety, to tell us when it's over. All normal broadcasting is suspended.

When the sky clears, the counting begins. We count the lives lost, the homes destroyed, the number of people without power, the dollar value of destruction. Dazed people are shown to us on TV, and asked to tell us their stories of miracles, near misses, and the loss of everything they owned.

I once followed the path of a particularly nasty tornado that had raked across the countryside and smashed through several small towns in its path. The towns were left mangled and bleeding, but in the open country between them it was difficult to find any evidence in nature of the storm's passing. The grass was green and lush just like before. Cows grazed, birds flew. The trees, having been pruned of their weaker branches, were stronger than ever. I could chart the storm's path, however, by the flattened barns and houses, the sheet metal and tufts of insulation flung against fences, the upside-down vehicles, the human detritus. Nature had barely seemed to notice.

I've been in two major dust storms pushed by sustained winds of 50-60 mph with gusts up to 80 mph. I was camping during one of them. I tethered my tent inside a thicket of cedars and hung on while the wind howled maniacally through a sleepless night. I drove five hundred miles the next day through a yellow haze with my lights on, past eighteen-wheelers lying on their sides, as every tumbleweed in the land passed me headed south.

Hurricanes in the Gulf routinely fling their remnants up over the plains.

Lightning once struck a tree across the street from my house as my family and I were arriving home in our pick-up. A limb landed in the truckbed. We were so stunned it took us a minute to realize what had happened. Leaves floated down around us as we got out of the truck and walked to the house in a daze.

We had an ice storm one winter that turned everything to crystals in the next day's cold bright sunshine. Trees crashed from the weight of the ice for days onto cars, roofs, and power lines. A TV transmission tower fell over. The electricity was out for eleven days in some neighborhoods.

One spring afternoon I witnessed something the weatherman called a "downburst." It was a unique event in my experience. A cloud became so heavily laden with water so quickly that it all came down at one time, in one place, pushing a shock wave down in front of the water. You couldn't call it rain. It destroyed a shopping center.

It seems there's always a car dealer around having a Hail Damage Sale.

But it's not all high drama. There are, of course, days when the sun-drenched sky is at room temperature and a mild breeze winnows through the flower gardens and the drone of lawnmowers near and far lulls you into a dreamless sleep in the backyard.

And there are gentle, nourishing rains that last for three days.

· · ·

I left Kansas City as the stormy night closed in. My only remaining quest was to get back to home and hearth in Tulsa. I drove through the night, with the windows down, drinking convenience store coffee and playing the radio really loudly. I watched the lightning off to the west and when I got bored with country music, I tuned into Big Bang music by switching the radio to AM and setting it between stations. This is something I often do driving late at night when it's easier to visualize the earth enveloped in a fuzzy ultraviolet-looking haze, hissing and popping with coded messages. Every radio is a decoder.

I'm fascinated by the pulsating, sine-waving white noise, and bits of obscure, overlapping voices from faraway places, in various languages. And by the scraps of melodies, familiar and unfamiliar, fading in and out to exotic, layered rhythms punctuated by the static sound of lightning. It's always there, the continuing sizzle of Radio's Big Bang, but you can hear it better at night. Of course, after a while it gives you a headache, so I switched back to country. Before long I found myself within reach of Tulsa's KVOO. Tangible evidence that I was rolling home. I listened to a Bob Wills tune, with God sitting in on percussion.

I skirted the stormy weather as I rolled south. I passed through Chanute, a place I'd once lived. My uncle Bill lives there still, and as I approached the road that leads to his house I was tempted to stop and beg a place to sleep the rest of the night. He's a kind man and wouldn't have minded. However, the hour was late, the road was empty, and my wife was expecting me, so I just honked my horn as I passed his road.

I passed through Coffeyville, the site of the famous last bank raid of the Dalton Gang. One day they rode into town from the west, and brazenly attempted to rob both of the town's banks at the same time. It was an audacious plan that failed miserably. The Daltons are buried outside of town. They gave Coffeyville the best day it ever had, its claim to fame, and the Dalton Museum is a popular shrine to them.

Tulsa drew ever closer, and I grew ever sleepier. I experimented with methods to keep myself awake as I drove along. Screaming as loudly as possible worked, but only fleetingly. Singing along with the radio was just too hard. I discovered the most effective method was to simply say my own name out loud, sharply, in the voice of my mother. I could get a good two minutes of alertness that way. I've used it since, and it works consistently. I recommend it. With every passing minute and mile the terrain became more familiar. I settled into a dull, semi-conscious state and let the car take over.

The lights of Tulsa came into view, and I sleep-drove down familiar streets, and finally pulled into my own driveway.

My wife was asleep on the couch, where she'd been waiting for me. "Hi, sweetie," she murmured when I awoke her.

"Hi," I mumbled. I roused her and walked her toward the bedroom. "I missed the harvest," I said, sitting on the edge of the bed.

"Well, maybe next year," she said, burrowing into the covers.

I turned out the light.

Maybe next year.

Spring rolled on, the prairie was bur

wheat turned a darker green

and began to ripple in the breeze.

Waiting for Harvest

July became August became September, then October.

Through the summer and fall I tried to make a living free-lancing with my camera and my computer, but nothing really worked well enough to pay the rent. I don't know if I'd lost my nerve, or my ambition, or if it was because there are a million guys out there with computers, and cameras, too, trying to make a living. Calling ourselves artists.

Maybe it was just that what I was really doing more than anything was waiting. Marking time until harvest came around again. I'd be ready this time, I told myself, and anyone else who'd listen.

Anyway, being unable to make enough profit to pay my fair share of the rent, I found myself in late November once again stranded on Route 66, employed by my loving wife in her newest diner, located right downtown, among the suits. I was a waiter now. In more ways than one.

In December, I read in the paper one Sunday that El Niño was expected off the coast of Peru any day.

It was a mild winter and on my days off I drove out to the country. Patches of winter wheat glowed vivid green in the brown and gray backdrop of winter. I took long walks along winding streams with my friend Flanagan in January and February.

"It's the year of El Niño," Flanagan said one day during one of our rambles. He kneeled close to the earth to carefully examine a rock that had caught his attention. He is an intense observer of nature.

"I've heard," I replied. I looked up at the winter sky, as if I could see El Niño in the clouds.

"They predicted it this year."

"It's right on schedule. The price of anchovies has gone through the roof, I've heard."

"It's raining in Houston right now. Hard. Really hard." He took out his camera and photographed the rock.

Back at the diner, early one rainy morning, I was looking through the newspaper and keeping an eye on the coffee cups of four guys at the counter who weren't in any hurry to work in the rain. Two salesmen, two carpenters.

The smell of fresh bread hung in the room. Mama had just left. She'd moved her baking operation to the new diner for its bigger kitchen.

Rain drummed against the plate glass windows. Something by the Four Tops played low on the radio.

"So, Rich," said Mark, one of the salesmen, "you gonna catch the harvest this year?" A smirk rippled its way down the counter through the four guys. My false start of the previous year was well known.

I looked up from my newspaper. "Yep. I'm just waiting for the wheat to ripen. Gonna be a while yet."

"'Nother month or so they'll be burnin' off the prairie up in the Flint Hills," said Dan, the other salesman. Burning the prairie is a springtime tradition in the Flint Hills and elsewhere. Dan grew up in the Flint Hills. "Harvest will be here before you know it," he added. "Got a job lined up yet?"

"No. There's plenty of time. Months yet." I looked out the window at the rain, then back at my newspaper. There was a front- page aerial photo of a Houston expressway under water for miles. It was a river, snaking off to the skyline on the horizon. Car tops here and there looked like stones in the river. El Niño, I thought.

"I did that once," said Dan, referring to the harvest.

"I know," I said. "You worked with Mexicans." I'd heard the story.

He twirled his empty coffee cup around on the counter. I ignored it.

"That's right," he continued, for the benefit of anyone who hadn't heard the story yet, "Mexicans. Me and one other guy were the only Americans on the crew. I was about seventeen at the time. This one Mexican seemed to be of the opinion that all Americans were lazy and soft. He was generous with his opinion. He was big for a Mexican, but I was big, too, and considered myself pretty tough. One day, when he mouthed off about Americans being soft and lazy I smacked him one right upside the head. Well, he smacked me right back. Made my ears ring. We commenced to rolling around in that wheat field, punching, biting, kicking, what have you, and you know what?" He directed his question at the carpenter sitting beside him.

The carpenter looked at the other carpenter, who was looking wistfully out the window, then he looked back at Dan. "What?" he said.

"Before long I began to realize that Mexican was right," Dan said. "Once I realized it, we quit fighting and got along pretty good after that."

"Damn this rain," said the carpenter who was looking out the window.

Spring rolled on, the prairie was burned, the wheat turned a darker green and began to ripple in the breeze. My spirits rose with the wheat.

I read long, scholarly books late at night on the history of wheat cultivation. I learned that animal husbandry and the cultivation of wheat both first occurred in the Tigris-Euphrates Valley at about the same time, about ten thousand years ago. I pointed this out to a customer as he spread butter over his toast with a rhythmic turning of his knife, a simple act. He answered me with a shrug.

A Brief History of Wheat Cultivation
and Its Civilizing Influence
Upon the Human Species

Mankind existed for thousands of centuries in one form or another as a species of hunter-gatherers. We kept on the move in small tribes, following our food sources, leaving behind virtually no traces of our passage. A dropped tool, a small quarry, our own bones, or footprints in the mud were pretty much the only things we left behind from all those millennia of wandering over the earth.

Our population was kept in check, like that of any other carnivore, by the population of our prey, and its food sources, and, like any other herbivore, by the abundance of wild plant food around us.

When a man awoke in the pre-dawn of those prehistoric days and stumbled outside the cave to take a leak, he faced the same question he'd faced the day before and the day before that: "Where will I find enough food today to feed my family?" The answering of that question dominated his mind and nearly monopolized his time.

The sun arched over the grassy plain, spreading life, and then disappeared behind low, dark hills. By then, if luck and skill had served the man, he lounged before the fire with his family for a while before they all drifted off to sleep with full bellies, to dream dreams we can't even begin to guess at.

If luck and skill hadn't been kind, if the question had gone unanswered, maybe a fitful night of little sleep ensued. Maybe he paced hungrily around the fire, past watchful women and sleeping babies. Maybe he went outside for a breath of fresh air (how fresh it must have been) to clear his simple mind and help him decide which direction to travel in the morning. Maybe he gazed up at the night sky as he asked again the unanswered question: "Where?" Maybe that was a prayer. And maybe then he lay himself wearily down in the fleshy warmth of his family and drifted off to sleep as the embers dimmed.

The next morning they moved on, confronted by the daily question—the only question—as blinding as the morning sun: "Where will we find enough food today?"

Among the plants that were part of prehistoric man's environment in the area we now call the Mideast, were two cereal grasses: Triticum dicoccoides, direct ancestor of emmer wheat, and Triticum aegilopoides, straight-line ancestor of einkorn wheat.

About eleven thousand years ago man began to leave behind a new set of tools in that area, such as flint sickle blades, grinding stones, and polished stone axes that, taken together, suggest partial subsistence on either wild grains or cultivated cereals. (From Karl Butzer, in *Prehistoric Agriculture*, edited by Stuart Struever, Natural History Press, 1971.)

Sometime between eleven thousand and nine thousand years ago—the record is murky—man began to cultivate wheat and barley in the Mideast. The domestication of sheep also occurred during this time. It would be difficult, if not impossible, to overstate the importance of this development in man's history.

At last the daily question had been answered, not just for a day, but for a season! The cultivation of wheat, along with the domestication of animals for food, provided a stable food supply, gave rise to permanent villages, and provided a degree of leisure time previously unimaginable.

Civilization began with the first wheat harvest.

By seven thousand B.C. farming was fairly widespread in the Mideast. Farming and villages arose hand in hand. Once a clan became attached to a specific site of farm land, and to spend their lives there, the concepts of land ownership and inheritance evolved. Villages formed. The village was a place to store and protect grain. Laws for the common good were developed. Village life provided a milieu for the birth of commerce, and specialization. And, since every day wasn't spent in a grim struggle to answer the question of where to find food, people were freed to consider other subjects.

To contemplate the shape of a hoe, the strength of an arch, the rolling of a wheel, the beauty of a sunset, the arc of an arrow, the raising of an army, the symbolism of money, the turning of the stars, the life-giving flow of water, the shape of a boat hull, the aesthetic possibilities in the loom's warp and weft, the improvement of wheat. And the writing down of their conclusions.

We operate under the belief that the ten thousand years we've spent building up civilization since that first wheat harvest insulate us with ten thousand layers from our primitive, animal past. But nothing breaks down civilization more quickly and completely than hunger.

Starvation is only days away from each of us. The loss of our humanity is just hours away, if we lose the answer to that most elemental question.

The sight of mountains of wheat piled up on the ground beyond our capacity to store it is...comforting.

. . .

There was a population explosion. Farmers, and the craftsmen they had spawned, spread far and wide, taking wheat and other crops with them. Wheat was introduced into areas where it had never grown indigenously. The concept of irrigation developed, and we began to leave indelible marks upon the land.

Selective breeding of wheat for desirable characteristics began to change domesticated wheat from its wild ancestor. In fact, as we have grown dependent upon wheat for survival, so has wheat become dependent upon us for survival. Wild grasses' seed pods are delicate things that shatter open with the least provocation to disperse their seeds. Humans have bred that property out of wheat, and other crops, because we want the seeds to be there for us to harvest. Modern wheat can't let go of its' seeds without our help. We need each other to survive.

Christopher Columbus introduced wheat to the New World. The natives of Mesoamerica had been farming corn, beans, and other native plants for centuries and had developed complex civilizations of their own. But the evolution of European civilization had been propelled by a hunger for knowledge, greed, and missionary zeal. This gave the Europeans a technological edge and the aggressive will to use it to steamroll the natives' civilizations right out of existence. The civilizations of Pre-Columbian America seem to have reached satisfactory conclusions about the universe and their place in it early on and they settled into a relatively static evolutionary pace.

The Spanish Conquistadors brought wheat north from Mexico into what is now the U.S. Southwest and California. Later, the Northern European settlers introduced wheat to the North American east coast.

And later still, Russian immigrants brought wheat with them to the Great Plains in the nineteenth century. More about them later.

Most of America's wheat is grown in the Great Plains, though wheat is grown in all regions of the country. Our wheat is divided into five major classes. Within those classes there are dozens, maybe hundreds, of breeds that have been developed by corporations and universities, each with its own set of properties of disease resistance, drought or moisture tolerance, maturation period, and other characteristics. The five major classes of wheat are:

> I. HARD RED WINTER WHEAT, grown primarily in the Southern and Central Plains. This is our most important wheat crop. In the 1990 crop year, according to the U. S. Wheat Associates 1990 Crop Quality Report, Hard Red Winter Wheat comprised slightly less than 45% of total U. S. wheat production. Hard Red Wheat is a bread wheat,

high in protein, and strong in gluten. It is used for yeast breads and hard rolls. It is sown in the fall and harvested in the spring.

2. HARD RED SPRING WHEAT, grown in the Northern Plains. This wheat comprised just over 20% of the 1990 crop. Hard Red Spring Wheat is also high in protein and gluten and is also used for yeast breads, and hard rolls.

3. DURUM WHEAT, grown in the Northern Plains. Durum is used for macaroni and spaghetti. In 1990, Durum wheat comprised only about 4% of total U. S. production.

4. WHITE WHEAT, grown in the Pacific Northwest, and the Northeast. White wheat is used for flat breads, cakes, pastries, crackers, and noodles. In 1990, it comprised a little more than 11% of U. S. totals.

5. SOFT RED WINTER WHEAT, grown in the South and the Central Lowlands east of the Great Plains. This wheat is used for flat breads, cakes, pastries, and crackers. It provided slightly less than 20% of total 1990 U. S. wheat production.

The Egyptians discovered that if wheat was ground and mixed with water into a dough, allowed to ferment, and then baked, they got bread.

. . .

One spring day I drove to Victoria, Kansas, to see a church erected by the Volga Germans, the Cathedral of the Plains. I took back roads and two-lane highways all the way. I drove through the Flint Hills east of Wichita and stopped in

El Dorado for lunch. The last forty or so miles to Victoria I was in the land of the stone fence post. The prairie there is abundant in outcropping limestone, and nearly devoid of wood so the ranchers long ago solved their fencing problems by hewing the stone into rude posts. Not surprisingly, they also built their buildings out of the same limestone. Crumbling stone ruins are a common sight in that country.

Victoria sits among the wheat fields like many other farm towns with its grain elevator along the railroad tracks. Usually the grain elevator in those towns is the tallest building, but in Victoria's case the elevator might be the second tallest, because the Cathedral of the Plains a few blocks north rises to an impressive height above the wheat and pastures and modest houses.

I made inquiries about the first settlers of Victoria, and was referred to the "town historian." I called his home and was told he wouldn't be home until evening.

I drove the short distance over to Hays and toured the old fort. In Hays I discovered a sculptor's studio. I strolled the sculpture garden in his back yard where he'd given a second life to many a derelict stone fence post by coercing lions, birds, women, and other living things out of their blunt shapes. I stayed in his garden until dark. Then I drove back to Victoria where I called the "town historian." We met at a convenience store by the highway and talked over coffee. He told me the story of his town's founding.

The story started in 1763 when Catherine the Great, Empress of Russia, issued an edict inviting the farmers of Germany to settle in Russia, where they would find arable land, exemption from the Russian Army, and freedom to practice their Catholic religion. There, on the Steppes of Russia, they farmed a wheat later known as Turkey Red, denoting its origin and color. This wheat was planted in the fall, grew slowly through the harsh winter, and was harvested in early summer.

By the early 1870s political conditions had changed and the "Volga Germans" as they were called, found their conscription exemptions and religious freedom threatened. Many of them emigrated from the Russian Steppes to the Great Plains of North America. They settled in central Kansas and formed farming villages with names from villages in their most recent homeland, names like Catherine, Pfeiffer, Liebenthal, Munjor, Schoenchen, and Herzog. They brought bags of Turkey Red Wheat with them. And also, it is said, they unintentionally brought with them seeds from a plant called Russian Thistle. We call it tumbleweed.

In 1873, a group of British aristocrats came to the plains and founded the village of Victoria, Kansas. They hired a London architect to lay out their streets, and began building fine estates. Their intention seems to have been to create a pastoral English country village on this bald plain.

Two years later, thirty-six families of Catholic Volga German peasant farmers arrived and daubed the good Kansas earth into a rude assemblage of mud huts just to the north of Victoria. They were well within sight of the fine ersatz estates of the aristocrats. The peasants named their modest settlement Herzog, after their village in Russia. They erected a large cross in the midst of their settlement, where they met to pray. They looked around at the fertile plains, not too different from the Steppes, and decided it was good.

Nice neighborhood, too, they must have thought, as they looked across the grass at the nicely laid out streets and expansive lawns of Victoria. They tilled the earth and sowed Hard Red Winter Wheat. They were there to stay, a fact not lost on their aristocratic neighbors to the south.

Within a few months all the genteel British aristocrats had vacated their still new premises, presumably to return to England, and a proper neighborhood.

The Russian peasants thus inherited a charming village of nice homes, named after the queen of England, and surrounded by fertile fields. Their American Dream was coming true: yellow wheat, blue skies, little white clouds, and nice, big empty houses. They sent for their relatives.

In time, through hard work and faith, the peasants prospered. The mud huts melted back into the earth. The simple cross they'd erected evolved into the magnificent Cathedral of the Plains. And they transformed the virgin prairie around them into a sea of thriving wheat fields that grew and grew. Across the street from the church is a statue of a Volga German family.

Today, Hard Red Winter Wheat is grown from the Rio Grande River in the south to the Cheyenne River in the north, and beyond. It accounts for about half of America's total wheat crop. Those pioneers' descendants are still living around Victoria, farming wheat descended from the original Turkey Red.

Just north of Victoria, near the old site of Herzog, is a cemetery. Those who came first, with their bags of seeds, have been laid down into the soil here by their children. Not a far journey, for they never rose that far above the soil in the first place.

It was well past dark when Victoria's town historian finished telling me his tale and I set out to drive back across four hundred miles of prairie to Tulsa. Late at night, listening to the white noise between stations, rolling alone over the dark earth beneath the stars, I heard a newscast in Spanish fade into hearing. I don't speak Spanish, but I kept hearing the words "El Niño" pop up into the monologue. Then the voice was drowned out in a tide of other frequencies, other voices, music.

The vision of simple clarity that had sustained me through

, hissing city winter was surprisingly elusive...

Hiring On

Harvest time was almost upon us. I began to look through small-town newspapers at the library for ads for harvest workers.

I answered an ad in the Enid newspaper that led to a job offer in Alva. Alva, it turns out, is home to a lot of custom harvesters.

The next day I drove out to Alva and met Alan Nusser, who was looking for a tractor driver. We looked each other over as I walked up to him in his equipment yard. I saw a man with thinning white hair and long, bushy sideburns, deep blue eyes behind glasses, a smooth complexion, and a sunny smile of all natural teeth. Average height, slender build, and an age impossible to guess.

I stated my business and we talked for a few minutes. At length he said yes, he'd give me a chance. He could use a tractor driver.

"I gotta tell ya, though, I don't allow no drinkin' nor drug abuse on my crews," he said. His blue eyes peered at me through his spectacles.

"No problem."

"Now, I mean none," he insisted.

"Okay."

"Awright, I just don't want there to be no misunder-standin's later on." He smiled a friendly smile, which I returned.

"Did you see my ad in the Alva paper?" he asked.

"No, I read it in the Enid paper."

His grin grew wider. "Well, I told the Alva paper to write 'Harvest help wanted. No drug or alcohol abusers need to apply.' They got 'er right except for one thing: they went an' left out the word 'no'! My phone's been ringin' off the hook all week!" he said. "Mostly just from my friends givin' me a hard time."

We laughed.

"We're plannin' to leave for harvest on the fourteenth of May," he said. "Be here any day that week, ready to go. We'll be gone until sometime in September, just dependin' on how it goes."

We shook hands and I drove back to Tulsa. I had about two weeks.

I spent the time framing houses with my brother-in-law. Hard outdoor work to get me physically geared up. I anticipated a summer of dust and sweat under the broiling plains sun. I expected to return to Tulsa after harvest with bronzed, leathery skin, sun-bleached hair and eyes, and lean from long days of hard, honest labor.

I'd forgotten about El Niño.

Debbie and the kids and I treated each other with unusual tenderness and respect as the time of my departure approached. One evening, I sat on the sofa in my study when Jennifer, my daughter, came into the room, quiet as a shadow, and gently insinuated herself under my arm. I put the book down.

"Hi," I said.

"Hi," she replied. "Wanna play some music?"

"'kay."

So I got out my guitar, and she got out her keyboard and we spent the rest of the evening happily making noise, and occasionally music, together. I sang her a song I'd written about living on the perfect street, in a town by the sea.

"That's nice," she said when I'd finished. "You named it after our street."

"Yeah. Wishful thinking, I guess."

"I'd like to live by the sea. Can I sing it while you play?" she asked. Jennifer loves to sing.

"Sure," I replied. I was flattered.

After my song she played a song she'd composed on her keyboard that incorporated bits of "Fur Elise" in the melody. I was impressed.

The next afternoon I was off work due to rain. My son Jared and I went to see an Arnold Schwarzenegger movie together. After the movie we sat in the mall "Food Court" sipping drinks, on Full Babe Alert.

"Woop, Woop, Woop!" Jared's alarm went off. "Two o'clock! Two o'clock! Two babes at two o'clock!" he urgently whispered their location. I set down my drink and picked up their reflection in his glasses. His eyes were bright with excitement. I turned discreetly around for a first-hand look.

"Jared, they're just kids!" I said. Jared's fourteen. I'm forty.

"Bull!" he replied, "Those are babes!"

A couple of minutes later my alarm went off. "Woop! Woop! Woop! Fox!" I hissed. "A definite fox, bearing 240 degrees, heading SSE!"

Jared sat up straight, alert, and checked my eyes to see where I was looking.

"Headed for the ice cream stand! Headed for the ice cream stand!"

He swiveled around in his seat. "Where? Who, her? Ewwwww! Are you kidding? She's older than Mom!"

"So what? She's a beautiful woman! Look at her!"

"Yeah. Right. For her age."

Just then both our alarms went off simultaneously. We looked around, straining in our seats, trying to get a bearing. It was strong, it was nearby. I, being older and more experienced, was the first to locate her.

"There!" I whispered excitedly. I pointed. "She's beautiful!"

Jared looked. His eyes widened. "Ohhh, perfect!" he sighed.

She glided past us toward the escalator, cool and aloof, a timeless vision of elegance, suppleness, and style in a sexy dress. She carried a bag that said "SHE." We locked in and tracked her progress. She disappeared slowly as she descended with the escalator.

We slumped back in our seats, sighing. Jared put his hand on his heart and looked toward heaven. "There is a God," he said.

We went off alert and finished our drinks, lost in thought.

As we walked across the pavement through the rain, on the way to the car, I put my hand on Jared's shoulder. "Jared," I said in a mock baritone, "take care of the womenfolk while I'm gone."

He nodded solemnly.

Debbie and I went out to Mary's Trattoria for dinner. We settled into our seats and ordered drinks.

Frank Sinatra's voice floated quietly in the air above us. There was a carnation on every table. We held hands and waited quietly for our drinks.

"So," I said.

"So," she agreed.

The owners of Mary's, Bruce and Sherry, are friends of ours. Sherry came to the table with drinks and menus.

"So, Rich, are you going to work the harvest this year?" she asked.

"Yes. I leave in a few days."

"Really? I was wondering...it's getting to be time, isn't it?" Sherry knows because she lived for several years in the wheat country.

We made small talk while Debbie and I looked over the menus. I ordered an antipasto appetizer. Debbie ordered a Caesar's salad.

"Are you really leaving?" Debbie asked me, somewhat rhetorically, with a soulful look.

"Looks like," I replied.

"We've never been apart that long."

"I know."

We chewed on breadsticks and sipped our drinks. We looked at the menus, though we both knew what we wanted.

"What if you don't want to come back?"

"Hey," I said quietly. I wanted to say the right thing, to reassure her, to let her know I loved her. "Hey," I repeated.

The appetizers arrived.

"It's scary," she said as she picked at her salad.

I swallowed my proscuitto and cheese. "Hey," I said again. I looked at her. "Do you really think our love is that fragile? That it would fall apart if we're absent each other's presence for a couple of months?"

Frank Sinatra and the boys finished up on a downbeat. There was a red carnation on every table. Glasses clinked.

"I love you," Debbie said.

Frank and the boys started up again, something lively.

I restrained myself as a matter of principle from saying "I love you, too." It robs the words of their sacredness and power to say them reflexively. Even though it was what she wanted to hear, and what I wanted to say, I would have to wait a few minutes. I guess I'm a romantic.

"Ready to order?" Sherry asked cheerfully a minute later, pen poised.

"Who's cookin'?" asked Debbie.

"Bruce."

"Oh, good. Pesto. Tell him it's for me. He'll know what to do."

"Right. Rich?"

"Fettucini Alfredo for me, Sherry."

"Awright." She walked away.

Later, as we pondered dessert, I said, "Will you be all right while I'm gone? It's not a great neighborhood we're in."

She looked up from the dessert menu. "Yeah. I'll be all right."

Tony Bennett began to sing. There was a red carnation in a Clearly Canadian bottle on every table.

"I love you," I said.

I stopped by my brother Michael's apartment the next day to say good-bye. He'd recently left his wife, and his place was decorated in Recently Single Male—an austere school. We made some small talk and lapsed into a comfortable silence that only brothers know.

A silence between two people in a room isn't just an absence of speech. It has nuance, texture, momentum. Two women in a room wouldn't be likely to understand the value of a good silence, and among men, no one understands it better than brothers.

At length, when the silence had run its full course and drawn to its logical conclusion, he spoke.

"So, you're going," he said.

"Yep."

He shook his head in mild disbelief.

We sat there for a while.

"Hey," he said, "I've got something I want you to hear." He stood up. "It's in the car," he said.

I followed him to his car. He put a tape in his deck and turned it up loud. Johnny French and the Public Defenders. We didn't speak for the next forty-five minutes.

"That was great!" I yelled when it was over. We got out of the car. "See ya!"

"See ya in the fall," he smiled.

When the day arrived, I packed up, said my good-byes, and drove west out of Tulsa. It was a warm, sunny morning. Debbie watched from our second-story bedroom window, waving sadly as I drove away. Her dog Max's face appeared in the window beside her.

I drove west toward Alva, deeper and deeper into wheat country. The wheat was a bright green-gold, not quite ripe. It rippled in the wind under a blue sky scattered with little white clouds. It was almost right.

The vision of simple clarity that had sustained me through the gritty, hissing city winter was surprisingly elusive, even then and there, deep in the wheat country, just before harvest. There were too many details, it seemed. Obscuring the yellow wheat, blue sky, and little white clouds would be a scruffy shelter belt, or an abandoned farmhouse, or a concrete elevator on the horizon, or a road.

I stopped once to photograph a scene. In the foreground the wheat rippled right up to the camera. A depression in the field receded diagonally toward the horizon. The horizon was obscured by a line of small trees which marked the passage of a dirt road, not visible in the photograph. What made the photograph worth taking for me was a small concrete bridge where the depression in the field curved into intersection with the unseen road. The small bridge arched low over the wheat.

I arrived at the Nussers' place in early afternoon. The rest of the crew were already there. They'd been on the job for a couple of days, getting the fleet ready for our extended journey. The workshop was a busy place. Two young men were working with a vise to replace a universal joint. Alan was under a trailer, welding on a wheel well. Another man, a little older than me and heavyset, was tracing the wires under the hood of a Ford pickup. I stuck my head under the hood.

"Hello," I said. "I'm Richard. What're you looking for?"

He looked up at me with large, bright blue eyes. "Hi, I'm Bill. I got a short here somewhere, or something. The headlights won't come on. You're the guy who drove out from Tulsa, eh?"

"Yep. I take it you checked the fuses."

"Checked the panel first thing. It was okay." He probed a wire with a test light. "I'm lookin' for a short somewhere now, or a blown in-line fuse. It's gotta be a fuse, seems like, because of the way it happened."

"What do you mean?" I asked as I looked around under the hood, ineffectually fingering the wiring.

"Well, she was working fine 'til I clamped the welder lead onto the bumper to ground it. That was all she wrote." He gave a little whistle, to simulate the sound of a falling bomb.

"Sure sounds like a fuse," I agreed. "Both headlights go out?"

"Yep."

"Everything else works?"

"Yep. Gotta be a fuse." He continued checking leads with the test light. He stretched his bulk over the fender.

I slipped around to the cab and stuck my head under the dash.

"Look if you like," he called out, "but we checked the panel first thing. Fuse number fifteen, right in the middle."

I looked at the fuse panel. Number fifteen was labeled "DOME ACCES. LAMPS." There was no fuse that said "HEADLIGHTS." I pulled fifteen out and looked at it. It was fine, of course, just as he'd said. I started to check the wiring to the switch, but fuse number seventeen caught my eye. It was labeled "RUNNING LIGHTS." Running lights. I took that to mean the amber lights across the top of the cab, and along the sides. I checked it anyway. It was blown.

"Hey, uh, Bill, I found it." I called out.

He popped out from under the hood. "Where?" he asked incredulously. He looked at the fuse I held up. "A fuse? But—"

"Number seventeen," I said. "Running lights."

"Running lights," he repeated. He came around and took the fuse from my hand and held it up to the light. He looked at me. "Number seventeen. Running lights," he mused, shaking his head. "Thought I checked that one, too."

We found a replacement fuse, plugged it in, and turned on the lights. They worked.

We walked over to help the other two men press in a new bearing in the u-joint. One of them was small, with dark hair and eyes. He held a hammer in his hand. He was missing one front tooth. His tee shirt was smeared with black grease. The other was tall, stocky, and fair. His eyes were hazel and his close-cropped hair was sandy blonde. He was holding the drive shaft to steady it in the vise. He wore a western shirt with snap buttons.

"Hi, I'm Richard," I said. "What's up?"

"I'm Jim," the small, dark one mumbled. He nodded and returned his attention to beating on the bearing with a hammer.

"I'm Luke," said the large, fair one. He wore a cap with the name of a sale barn in Missouri on it.

"You guys need any help?" I asked.

"Sure!" said Luke. "Pile on in here."

Soon we were all four doing what was obviously a two-man job. Luke and I both steadied the drive shaft, along with the vise. Bill held a pipe against the bearing, and Jim tapped it with the hammer.

Alan finished welding and walked over. "You fellers got 'er outnumbered?" he grinned.

We all agreed that we did. Jim tapped the bearing home.

"I see ya made it," Alan said to me.

"Oh, yes. Wouldn't have missed it."

"Oh, hey, boss!" Bill said, "We got that headlight problem fixed. It was a fuse after all. Number seventeen."

"Seventeen? Hmm. Thought we checked that one."

We spent the rest of the day doing various last-minute preparations.

About five-thirty Alan's wife Leota appeared in the shop door and informed us that supper was ready.

We followed her around to a travel trailer at the side of the building and lined up at the door. She handed each of us a plate of supper and a glass of tea. Behind her, two easy chairs sat facing the TV, which was on.

I followed the other hands over to a second, much older travel trailer where we ate. This trailer was a 1954 Spartan trailer home modified into a four-man bunkhouse. It had a TV and a stereo in the main room. It was also equipped with a washer and dryer, refrigerator, freezer, sink, pantry, toilet, shower, and in the tiny bedroom, four bunks.

After supper I stowed my gear in the trailer and walked around the yard and looked over the fleet: two Ford 9000 diesel- straight, tandem-axle grain trucks, one long nose, one snub nose; two John Deere combines, one model 9600 and one 8820; two thirty-foot combine headers on a trailer; one John Deere 4640 tractor hitched to a grain cart; the combines and tractor and grain cart were all on custom trailers; also, one Ford semi-tractor with a grain trailer; a Ford one-and-a-half-ton service pickup with a 200-gallon fuel tank in the bed; two more Ford pickups; and the two travel trailers.

Evening fell as Luke, Jim, and I settled into our new home. We turned on the TV. Bill had gone home to spend one last night with his wife. He and Jim were local men. Luke was from just outside Branson, Missouri.

We could only get one channel—the PBS channel. There was a documentary about a crew of men from Norman who chase tornadoes in a van. Their goal is to put themselves in the path of a tornado and set down a torna-do-proof metal drum filled with measuring equipment and a homing device, and flee. There was some exciting footage of rampaging tornadoes. One of the meteorologists said, "There's always been much disagreement about where the Great Plains begins when you come at it from the east. I would say this: You know you're in the Great Plains when you can no longer ignore the sky."

We turned off the TV when "Masterpiece Theater" came on. I went to bed, though not to sleep, just to think. I lay there in the darkness and listened to the crickets. There was a powerful, moving denseness to their throbbing song.

In the living room Luke and Jim scanned the FM air-waves for some rock and roll. I heard a radio voice say, "El Niño, or Pinatubo? Stay with us..." but they didn't, search-ing as they were for three chords with a back beat, and lust-inspired lyrics. All they could find was country. "Ah don't mind country," I heard Luke say in his lilting Ozark drawl. "That's jist not what Ah'm in the mood for right now. Ah wanna rock! Aaoooh!"

In a few minutes the radio went off and the front door slammed. I heard Jim's car start up and pull away.

I was alone with millions of crickets.

Our sense of the passage of time became more and more va

th no particular time to get up in the morning,

and days of semi-darkness.

$\mathcal{S}$outh of the Red River

The next morning Bill woke us just before sunrise. We rolled out of our bunks, dressed, and stepped outside, eager to break camp and start down the road. It had rained during the night. The camp was puddled, and the sky was a confused mess of rushing clouds, patches of blue, and early slanting light. A flock of egrets flew over the camp. The air was cool and damp.

Alan and Leota own a nice house in a nice part of Alva, but since they'd already shut it down for the summer, they'd spent the night in their trailer next to us. We broke camp after a simple breakfast.

Bill was adrenaline-driven, officiously hustling his bulk around from truck to truck, plowing through puddles, shouting orders, tightening this, checking that, urging the rest of us to hurry. Soon, we'd hooked up the travel trailers, fired up the diesels, and pulled out in convoy, headed south.

Alan took the lead in the semi, pulling the tractor and grain cart; then came Leota, pulling their trailer behind a pickup; then Jim, pulling our trailer behind a pickup; then Luke, driving one of the grain trucks, and pulling a combine; then me. I drove the service truck, and pulled the combine headers. Bill brought up the rear, driving the other grain truck, and pulling the other combine.

We drove south on U.S. 281 to Seiling, where we got onto U.S. 183. The trail now took us nearly due south to the Red River through Clinton and Frederick. Highway 183 is a major route for custom harvesters, right through the heart of the wheat country. We encountered several other harvest caravans along the way. Alan and Leota chatted over the two-way radios about the other crews. They seemed to know them all. The deeply rumpled landscape was supremely beautiful in the morning light. The more level areas were planted in large tracts of waving wheat, shaped by the topography. Cattle grazed peacefully on the grassy hillsides.

Jim took the lead outside Frederick so he could cross the Red River first and block traffic at the other end of the bridge for our wide loads. We crossed the Red River just downstream from its confluence with the Pease River.

Some twenty miles upstream on the Red as the crow flies was the site of Doan's Crossing. Doan's Crossing is where the old Great Western, or Texas-Ogallala, cattle trail crossed the Red into Indian Territory. It isn't shown on modern maps but it was once an important river crossing. Doan's store served the cowboys, and others who forded the river there, with supplies, mail, and a ferry.

We proceeded south and east through Electra and Mankins, and then into the small town of Holliday, our destination. We pulled into a campground on the west end of town where Alan and Leota had stayed on previous trips. The shakedown cruise had gone uneventfully.

We all got out to stretch. Alan looked over the campsites

and decided where to park the bunkhouse and his quarters. He pulled his trailer into place and told Bill to pull the bunkhouse up over the curb into its spot. Then he walked over to his trailer to hook up his plumbing.

Bill jumped in the pickup. Luke and I stood on the outside, the driver's side of Bill's projected curve. Jim walked over to the passenger side, to watch the inside of the curve as Bill turned the pickup into the curb to climb it and pull the forty-foot bunkhouse up off the street and onto the grass.

Before any of us was quite ready, Bill had cut his wheels and pulled the pickup's front tires up onto the grass. As he pulled the pickup's rear tires up onto the curb, one at a time, we heard a tearing sound. Bill hit the brakes.

"Whoa," said Jim, quietly. He raised his hand half-heartedly, knowing it was too late. The back bumper of the truck had punctured the aluminum skin of the bunkhouse right before his eyes. Bill had turned too sharp. Jim hadn't warned him. Luke, Bill and I stepped over to Jim's side of the truck to survey the damage. We all stood there staring at the hole. No one spoke. Alan walked over to see what the problem was.

"Well, I swear!" he exclaimed. "I had four men on this little job and you all still managed to go and put a hole in my trailer. Bill! What the hell? What do you have to say?"

Bill bowed his head.

"I want to know how this happened!" Alan continued. "What's the matter? Can't anybody speak? Have you all been struck dumb?"

We stood there in a row, glancing at the tear, and studying our shoe tops, as if we might find some answer there. In fact I think we had been struck dumb, in a way. No one answered Alan even with a shrug. We couldn't. It was impossible to speak. We just stood there waiting for whatever came next. This was the first time I'd seen Alan angry.

"Well, I'm glad I didn't have eight men!" Alan said, at last, as he walked over to get into the pickup and park the bunkhouse himself. "There's no tellin' how much damage you'd've done with eight of you watchin' out!" He parked the trailer with ease, and with four very alert men watching every move the truck and trailer made under his control.

When he got the trailer parked, Alan jumped out of the truck and said to us, "Come on! Let's go eat before you all tear somethin' else up!" He started walking down the street to the L&R Cafe. The rest of us followed in silence a few steps behind him.

The L&R Cafe in Holliday is a modest cinder-block building. A slew of pickups with fuel tanks in the beds crowded around it. We walked in and sat down. The walls were of rough-cut pine planks. On a board above the door the proprietors had apparently tried to start a collection of cattle brands from their customers, but so far only two brands had been burned into the wood.

We were just about the only men in the place not wearing spurs.

The waitress, a small, spare woman, slipped through the cowboys to our table.

"Here's your menus," she said. "Y'all want some tea?"

We nodded in unison.

"Y'all harvesters?" she asked.

We nodded.

"We figured it was gettin' about harvest time," she said and walked away to get our drinks.

We ate in virtual silence amid the cowboy hubbub. I took a couple of stabs at engaging Bill in conversation but it went nowhere. It was as if, having so recently been struck dumb, we were going to have to learn to talk all over again.

Alan's anger had subsided and he made small talk with a local man who recognized him from previous harvests.

After lunch we finished setting up camp, which eventually got us all talking again. Bill and Alan drove out to the fields to look the crop over.

"Alan says it looks like the wheat'll be ready in two or three days!" Bill reported when they returned.

This news was greeted by us all with enthusiasm. We were all eager to get into the field and start the harvest.

The next morning the sun peeped over the horizon like a thief peeping over a windowsill. Almost immediately a thick blanket of sullen, low clouds rushed over us and, in effect, pulled the shade. By 8:00 a.m. we were looking out the bunkhouse window at a pouring rain, accompanied by thunder and lightning.

"Well," Bill surmised, "if it clears up tomorrow, the fields will dry up just about the time the wheat gets ready. If it clears up tomorrow."

We turned on the TV to catch the forecast. After a short wait, the Wichita Falls weatherman showed us a satellite view of a swath of clouds swooping up out of the Gulf of Mexico, obscuring the entire southern plains in a graceful arc, all the way up to the Arkansas River valley.

"No end in sight," I heard the weatherman say. "Right on through the weekend, and into next week."

It rained eighteen of the next twenty-three days. We only got into the field long enough to harvest 160 acres of the two thousand or so we had scheduled. The rest of the time we spent playing poker, watching TV, sipping coffee at the L&R Cafe, sleeping, or staring out the window of our little trailer. I also spent a lot of time standing under the eaves of the convenience store across the street talking to Debbie on the pay phone, pressed against the wall to keep dry.

The rains were long and heavy, falling from mountainous thunderheads that rolled in every afternoon, or from a solid, amorphous, low blanket in the morning. We lived in twilight most of the time. The sunlight was diluted, drained of color and nuance, filtered through low, moving clouds. The sandy ground became saturated and rainwater spread out around us in standing pools. Frogs croaked all day. Mosquitoes flourished.

"Sumbitch," said Luke one day. He'd just cleaned Jim and me out in poker and was scraping his winnings into a coffee can. The rain beat on the roof in rhyme to the clinking of change going into his can. "I come out here expectin' hard work under the hot sun."

"I know," I said, "I was gonna go home with skin like

leather, bronzed by the sun." I watched my quarters, dimes, and nickels disappear into his coffee can.

"Yeah, bronzed," Luke agreed. "Lean and hard."

"Glistening with sweat."

"Sweaty, right—and covered with chaff."

"Covered with chaff?" I asked.

"Hey, chicks dig guys with chaff!" he assured me. "Makes 'em crazy!" Luke had been raised by his grandfather on a cattle farm on the north slope of the Ozarks. His grandfather, as described by Luke, was a cow-tradin', straight-shootin', hard-drinkin', woman-chasin' farmer of a man. Luke had learned about animal husbandry at an early age. He was sure he knew what chicks liked. He'd been making a living since high school cutting and hauling hay, so maybe he knew about chaff, too.

"Makes 'em crazy, eh?" I asked, intrigued.

"Oh, yeah! They love it! But, hell, look at this!" He lifted up his teeshirt and showed Jim and me his pale, soft belly. "I feel like a damn salamander!" he said, inspecting his navel for lint.

"Aw, quit yer bitchin'," said Bill from across the room. (In our trailer, across the room was about three feet away.) "I'm tryin' to watch 'Bonanza!'"

Jim looked silently out the window.

The first week or so, we'd all followed Bill outside whenever the rain let up, as he compulsively searched for busywork to perform on the trucks and equipment. Eventually, when we were reduced to rearranging nuts and bolts, even he had given up.

Our sense of the passage of time became more and more vague, with no particular time to get up in the morning, and days of semi-darkness. Our sleeping habits changed. We'd pad around the trailer at all hours, quiet and pale as ghosts. We were as likely to be asleep at noon as midnight. We'd pass each other at 3:00 a.m. illuminated by the flickering glow of a televised car chase, the sound turned almost all the way off, the squealing tires and gunfire barely audible.

"What time is it?" I'd mumble.

"Who knows?" came the murmured reply. "What day is it?"

"Who cares?" I'd shuffle down the hall.

Luke, the youngest, amazed the rest of us with the amount of time he spent sleeping, day and night.

Jim, who rarely spoke anyway, began to only mumble, inaudibly and infrequently. If you asked him to repeat himself he would yell. He was obviously yelling, by the pitch and timbre of his voice and the strained expression on his face, but not by his volume, which only reached normal conversational levels.

I began to take long, moody walks down the railroad tracks when the weather allowed, past abandoned oil fields. Mesquite jungles dominate the landscape around there, alternating with wheat fields. I read in the Wichita Falls newspaper that mesquite isn't native to that part of the plains, but moved in opportunistically as a result of severe, prolonged overgrazing, which killed out most of the native grasses, in the late nineteenth and early twentieth centuries. I saw my first jackrabbit on one of those walks. I was standing stock still in plain sight, and he hopped silently almost right over my foot. I don't think he ever saw me.

Bill buried himself in an intensive study of the early works of Red Sovine. For entertainment he searched for old westerns on TV. He always kept one eye trained on Alan's door, visible outside our window from his TV chair.

Bill had spent twenty years on the flight line for the Strategic Air Command servicing B-52s. Even though the SAC was taken off alert several years after Bill retired, Bill had never really come off alert.

One day I was sitting at the table in the living room reading when Alan walked across the muddy yard from his trailer to ours. He leaned his head in the door, and said to me in a stage whisper, "Are they all a sleepin'?"

"Yes," I said. I was the only one out of bed.

"Well, when they get up and around, tell 'em I want to move those trucks sometime today. I don't care who does it and there's no hurry, just whenever," he said quietly.

"Okay," I replied.

He closed the door and walked toward his pickup.

I leaned over to put on my shoes and go move the trucks.

Just as I got hold of my shoe I heard a mighty thump in Bill's room. Out he came, fully dressed and shod as he barreled right past me. He nearly trampled me as he lunged for the door and threw it open. He leaped out with a hearty cry of "Hey, boss!"

Twenty years in the SAC will do that to a man.

Over the days and weeks of idleness, Alan became more and more agitated. It was understandable, because he had a huge investment in equipment that was sitting idle. The two combines alone were in the range of one hundred thousand dollars each.

And the payroll just kept rolling along. He couldn't believe his bad fortune. "I've never seen anything like it," he said sadly, over and over again. He wasn't alone. There were harvest crews camped all over Holliday, and for that matter, all over north Texas, all in the same swamped boat.

The waitress at the L&R shook her head sympathetically as she poured coffee for tables full of idle men.

"What're y'all doin' over there in them trailers all day?" she asked. "Y'all must be gettin' stir crazy by now!"

"I'm gettin' hooked on soap operas!" an able-bodied man lamented.

"My goodness." she shook her head sadly at the idea of men being forced by idleness to watch soap operas all afternoon. She, on the other hand, was forced by her labors to miss them. "'Course, this rain's no picnic for the farmers, either," she pointed out. She knew most of the area farmers personally. Some of them were usually sitting around in the cafe with us, talking about the endless rain.

The wheat ripened and then over-ripened while we waited for the rains to stop long enough for the fields to dry. When the wheat began to sprout in the head, Alan and the other harvesters began to look northward, where the wheat was ripening and the fields were drier.

The farmers were facing the prospect of having to let a good crop rot in the fields, which is by and large what happened. Their reactions ranged from panic to resignation, by way of anger and bitterness.

The rain kept falling.

One payday our crew drove into Wichita Falls to shop, which was a depressing experience. Wichita Falls seemed like a bedroom community that had come unmoored and drifted off by itself and had to become self-sufficient. All the uninspired, mind-deadening, familiar elements of a modern American city were there, counterbalanced by nothing which allowed me to identify Wichita Falls as a specific place. It looked like many another American city, with the rotting downtown core, the strips of malls and franchise restaurants, the tract houses. The network TV affiliates, the classic rock FM station, and the expressways. The check-cashing places, the pawnshops, and the striptease joints. It reminded me of everywhere I'd ever wanted to leave. Or maybe I was just feeling surly.

We had supper while we were in town. I was driving so I picked the place. I kept driving until I spotted a place that looked like it might not have a corporate office in Dallas.

Luke became morose as soon as we sat down. The place was full of cheerful people hoisting frosty mugs of beer over baskets of french fries and the like. Pretty, young, snake-hipped waitresses wearing shorts and tee shirts twisted and squeezed past our table and through the room swinging full trays over our heads. When our waitress came to take our order, Luke turned sullen and said he didn't want anything. The rest of us ordered cheeseburgers and iced tea.

"What's the matter?" I asked him after she'd delivered our tea. "Don't you like this place?"

"The only two things I want are all around me and I cain't have neither one of 'em!" Luke complained.

"What two things?" I asked, although I had a pretty good idea. We'd been away from home for a while.

"Beer and pussy," Luke said grimly. "This is jist all so lame!" he gestured around our table at us, his compadres. We chastely sipped at our iced teas.

I can only surmise what he must have seen in us: a sawed-off stoic with a missing front tooth, a fat-man lackey, and me, an old married city slicker who'd taken a vow not to drink. I noticed that my pinky had extended itself. I snapped it back into place around my tea glass.

"Man, every harvest crew I've ever heard of was a buncha partyin' fools!" Luke continued his lament. "Work hard, play hard, drive the company truck into the ditch with a buncha underage local girls, and then move on north to the next town! This is lame!" He stared hard into his glass of ice water and spoke no more.

Luke was only twenty years old, in the middle of the age of overindulgence. He'd anticipated this summer in the fields as the latest location of his moveable feast, but it was turning out to be nothing more than prolonged coitus interruptus. Bill smiled benignly. He'd gotten a haircut recently, a burr. In the light of the room he looked a little like Uncle Fester from the Addams Family. Jim gazed up at a football game on a big-screen TV in the corner. With his tongue he worried the hole where his front tooth used to be. He seemed not to be watching the game, but just looking at the flickering light, like a cat.

It was pretty lame, I had to admit. I, and maybe Jim, too, would have loved a cold beer or two, instead of tea, but Alan was a teetotaler and we'd all understood that we weren't to drink alcohol while in his employ. Bill, Alan's right-hand man, his sidekick—and our constant companion—was also a teetotaler.

We'd all probably have loved some pussy by then, too, but, being the youngest, Luke suffered the most. I shook my head sympathetically. I couldn't console him.

. . .

On the way back to Holliday we passed a roadhouse. A sign outside said "CALICO INN CATFISH FRY THIS SAT. NITE LIVE MUSIC 'TEXAS HEAT'." I decided to go.

At the Holliday city limits there's a Texas State Historical Marker. I asked Bill, who'd taken over driving, to pull over so we could read it.

I've always been a sucker for historical markers. This one told the story of Captain Jack Holliday, and how the town was named after him. His story went something like this, though I'm only telling it from memory:

Jack Holliday was born early in the nineteenth century and raised in Holliday, Pennsylvania, a town his great-grandfather had founded. When he was still a young man he quit his job in the town's blacksmith shop and rode a horse west. Within a couple of years he'd made it to Texas, just in time to get caught up in Texas' fight for independence from Mexico. He volunteered and was made a captain. Captain Jack Holliday. It had a nice ring to it.

During the war he and his men were part of an expeditionary force sent to capture Santa Fe. They marched west along a buffalo hunters' trail. At one of their campsites en route Captain Jack carved his name in a tree. The next day they moved on.

When they got to Santa Fe, they were trounced by the Mexicans and Captain Jack and the others who weren't killed were captured and marched to Mexico City. There they languished in a Mexican prison, dying a few at a time of dysentery, malaria, and other tropical diseases.

Jack, however, survived, and after two years he was released. Mexico had lost the war, and Texas was an independent country. Jack and the other survivors, sick and weak, were loaded on a ship at Veracruz and shipped north. They were bound for Galveston and freedom in a nation of their own making.

Jack never made it. He died aboard ship and was thrown into the Gulf of Mexico.

After Jack had lain at the bottom of the sea for some fifty years, and Texas had given up its independence and emerged, after an unfortunate decade or so, as a member in good standing of the USA, a group of pioneer entrepreneurs decided to start a town on the north Texas prairie.

They chose a site along an old buffalo bone gatherers' trail near Jack's campsite of over a half-century earlier, and began developing lots.

All they needed was a name for their new town. They thought and thought, but nothing sounded quite right. They wanted something simple, something cheerful, something inviting, to promote the place to prospective visitors and settlers. One day a group of men was gathering wood and saw the name "Capt. Jack Holliday" carved into a tree. Right away they knew they'd found the name for their town: Holliday. Holliday, Texas. Holliday, Texas, USA. And so it was. And so it is.

Captain Jack Holliday, formerly of Pennsylvania, never knew that his name would outlive him, outlive the tree, and outlive the nation he died helping to create. And the men who'd honored him by naming their town after him never knew a thing about Captain Jack Holliday, except that his name had a nice ring to it.

Later that evening I walked across the street (formerly a buffalo bone hunters' trail) to the convenience store to call Debbie on the pay phone. Max, her dog, barked impatiently in the background while we spoke. We arranged a conjugal visit for the middle of the following week. It was our anniversary.

"I gotta go, sweetie!" Debbie said after we'd decided day and time, "Mama don't feel good, so I have to go in early and bake the bread! Love you! See you next week! You better be ready! Bye!"

I spent the next few days in a state of double anticipation. Saturday night was the fish fry, with a live band at Calico Inn, and the next Tuesday was Debbie, in all her femaleness, driving all the way from Tulsa to be with me for a night. Wine, women, and song, as they say. Two out of three ain't bad.

Saturday night came and Bill drove me the four miles up the road to Calico Inn and dropped me off. The festivities were already well under way. A group of men and women were gathered around a camp range on a folding table outside by the front door, frying and eating catfish and pulling longnecks out of a stock tank full of ice and beer. The band was tuning up inside.

The Calico Inn is a squat cinder-block building about twice

as long as it is wide. In the center of the building a bar runs lengthwise. At the west end of the bar is a dance floor and bandstand. At the east end are pool tables and the restrooms. Behind the bar is a room full of beer. Tables are squeezed in wherever.

A fair-sized crowd of happy people chewing on greasy catfish and sucking on longnecks called out to one another from underneath their cowboy hats and puffy hairdos. I settled in at the end of the bar nearest the band, ordered a Seven-Up, and waited for the music to begin, which is what I was there for.

Just before the band started a couple of men from the harvest crew camped next to us walked in. They recognized me and squeezed in at the end of the bar beside me. Pat and Slim. Pat's from Los Angeles, where he works as a truck driver, delivering luxury automobiles to dealers all over the country. Every year, however, his employer gives him a leave of absence to work the harvest. He told me he needs to get out on the plains, where he grew up, as an antidote to L.A.

Slim ordered a beer and proceeded to tell me his life story, which took the rest of the night. He never stopped talking longer than it took to take a drink. The band started playing at about the same time he started talking, so all I caught (between songs) of his epic tale was that his name was Slim, he was from Texas, and he was "just an ol' bull hauler" until some unfortunate alcohol/traffic incident ended his bull haulin' days, at least for now.

The band was as great as I'd hoped they would be. Their repertoire included all the recent country hits and lots of Texas blues, a la Stevie Ray. They were suitably loud, bending and twisting those familiar three chords all over the room, fronted by a lead guitar player with the power, precision, and passion to knock a man's cowboy hat off and steal his girlfriend, at thirty paces. He was good, really good.

But I knew he'd never be famous. I hoped he didn't mind.

As the night wore on the crowd grew and got happier and happier from the beer, and greasier and greasier from the catfish. People belly to belly and shoulder to shoulder, with glittering eyes and shiny chins, grinned and guzzled. The dance floor filled and emptied on a musical tide. People yelled out to each other over the music. Sometimes they yelled words, and sometimes they just yelled. The smell of catfish, alcohol, and tobacco filled the air, with a possible faint hint of marijuana occasionally detectable.

I nursed my Seven-Up and enjoyed myself. Slim continued his unheard monologue, which I encouraged by an occasional nod in his direction.

At one point an angel, an actual honky-tonk angel, sat down beside me at the bar, an actual tragic honky-tonk angel. She ordered the first of several Pinatubo Sunsets, and started pumping quarters into a poker vending machine on the bar before her. She won forty million dollars. Still, she didn't seem happy.

Eventually the catfish ran out, the band exhausted its repertoire twice, and the night came to a close. Our dulled ears heard car doors slam in the parking lot, cars and pickups coughing reluctantly to life, throwing gravel. Pat and Slim were too drunk to drive so I drove them home, which worked out well for all of us.

The next morning, the sun was up at the crack of dawn, arcing purposefully up into a pristine sky, getting on with its day, and rousing the rest of us to do the same. We tumbled out of the trailer, squinting and looking around at a world full of intense colors.

By noon the ground had dried enough that Alan decided we would try to cut some wheat. We eagerly piled into the pickup and drove out to the fields, where the combines and tractor had waited for us for so long. I looked around from the cab of my tractor at a world of yellow wheat, blue sky and little white puffy clouds. It would have been perfect except for the mesquite jungle pressing up against the wheat field. We made a few rounds that day, working our way around the mud holes, and more rounds the next day, which was also bright and sunny.

When we'd gotten all we could from the first field we moved down the road to the next one and got what we could there. We had better luck in the second field, because it was high and well drained. We worked until well after dark, and went home tired and happy. We'd earned our keep that day.

That was pretty much the extent of our wheat cutting south of the Red River, because the rain returned the next day.

Tuesday morning it was still raining but by Tuesday afternoon the sun came out. We couldn't work the fields so we spent the sunny afternoon playing croquet on the soggy lawn.

Debbie arrived just before supper. What a pleasure it was to see her big blue Ford van come splashing through the puddles. Her dog Max was sitting upright in the passenger seat. I quickly gathered up my bag and headed out, waving good-bye over my shoulder as the screen door slammed behind me. She was all smiles, and I guess I was, too.

"Happy anniversary!" she said.

"Same to ya!"

Max thoroughly sniffed me.

Alan had given me the next two days off, so we headed to Fort Worth. We made it about thirty miles before we pulled off beside a muddy cornfield and gave each other a proper hello. We kept bumping against the horn, but we didn't care.

We spent the night getting reacquainted in some cheap motel on the outskirts of Fort Worth.

Next day I bought her a book at the Botanical Gardens as her anniversary gift. We went downtown and she bought me a straw Stetson as my gift. I wore it proudly out of the store, catching my reflection in the shop windows, until we turned a corner and it blew off. I had to chase my new hat across a busy street.

That afternoon we checked into a nicer motel. Our plan was to go out for dinner and maybe dancing if we felt like it. Then back to the motel. But first Debbie wanted to buy some sexy underthings so after we checked in we went to a nearby mall. The mall was nestled into the side of an enormous, complex interchange of expressways and service roads connecting Dallas, Fort Worth, and the airport.

We left Max in the van with the window rolled down part way so he'd have air. When we got back to the van he was gone.

As we looked across the acres of parking lot and further,

to the knot of highways all around, the color drained from Debbie's face.

We spent the next four hours searching the area, calling out his name, accosting strangers, driving slowly in ever-widening loops as the sultry afternoon gave way to sultry night.

We separated. I drove slowly along the expressway, peering grimly down at the roadside as cars and trucks rushed past me, blaring their horns. About two miles west of the knot of ramps, feeders, thru-lanes, under- and overpasses, grassy islands, and swooping arcs of pavement that constituted the sprawling interchange I saw his body. He was lying near the rail, halfway across a bridge over a side street.

I drove to the first exit, another two miles, and worked my way back through the neighborhood, through a tortuous maze of one-way streets and cul-de-sacs. At last I arrived under the overpass where Max lay, and pulled the van over onto the curb. I got out and scaled the steep, grassy embankment to the elevated roadside.

The traffic hurtled by with unforgiving violence, pinning me, in effect, between the painted line and the guardrail.

It was clear what had happened. Max, lost and confused, had run down the highway until he got to the bridge and, in his innocence, had tried to cross it. He'd made it nearly halfway. There wasn't even room for his slender body between the bridge rail and the line that marked the edge of the traffic lane. He lay on his side with his stiff legs sticking out into the roadway.

I stood there, pressed between the road and the guardrail, blasted by the roar, the wind, and the glare of the oncoming traffic, and waited for a pause in the flow. When I thought I could make it, I would run to the middle of the bridge, get Max and carry him back to the safety of the embankment.

I would try not to get trapped on the bridge as Max had.

The air was thick and damp. I was soaked with foul-smelling sweat. My clothes stuck to me. My feet swam inside my shoes.

About one-eighth mile upstream the highway curved out of sight. I waited until the traffic thundering past me broke up momentarily and left the road empty between me and the curve.

I ran onto the bridge, watching closely behind me. Just before I reached Max, a knot of bouncing headlights shot out around the bend, and bore ruthlessly down on me. I scooped Max up in my arms. He was cold; colder, it seemed, than a merely inanimate object, and heavier. There was little blood. With Max in my arms I ran as fast as I could in the eight-inch space between the bridge rail and the traffic lane. I raced straight toward the oncoming traffic, toward the bridgehead and safety, gulping in the thick air.

I made the bridgehead with less than a second to spare, as the cluster of trucks and cars bellowed past me and my burden.

I stepped heavily over the low guardrail to the safe, relatively serene, grassy bank. I laid him down in the grass, and sat beside him for a minute to catch my breath. Then I ran down the bank to the van and drove with reckless abandon to find Debbie. How could I have left her alone in such a brutal place?

When I found her she was talking to a policeman. They both seemed relieved to see me. I told her I'd found him and that he was dead. She cried until we got back to the grassy bank, to his body, and then, depressed and exhausted, she sank into silence. We wrapped the body in a blanket and loaded it into the van and drove to the motel. It was a little after midnight. Debbie called her mother in Tulsa and cried to her while I ran a tub full of hot water.

I bathed her slowly and thoroughly until she was calm and clean. We hardly spoke. I had to spend a long time on her feet, as she'd been barefoot much of the night. I led her to bed. She struggled for comfort while I poured myself a bath.

After I'd bathed I sank like a ship into her storm-tossed bed. We slept the dreamless, exhausting sleep of motels.

. . .

We awoke the next morning to a heavy, pounding rain. It drummed on the roof of the motel while we lay in bed staring morosely at the big, creeping blot over the Southern Plains on the weather channel. I slipped on my new cowboy hat and old blue jeans and dashed outside shirtless and barefoot to get a clean shirt from the van. Rain pummeled the van roof as I ducked into it. Max lay shrouded and still in a rear corner, but his presence filled the space to overflowing. I quickly backed out into the rain with my clean shirt. Rain streamed off the brim of my hat as I stepped back into the room.

We checked out and headed north on Highway 287.

The hard rain finally stopped. We drove back to Holliday through clouds snagging their soft bellies on the low plains and seeping mist over the land. Creeks were inches from flowing over the pavement. At one point I saw a patch of sunlight by the horizon so diffused and soft, filtered through the low clouds, that it didn't throw shadows. The land and objects on its surface seemed to glow from within.

Debbie dropped me off at the Nussers' camp, and after a sad good-bye she drove away.

The guys, lounging around the trailer like lizards, roused up at my arrival and looked me over casually for indications of having been recently laid. There were none. I told them all about Max. They told me they'd cut a little wheat while I was gone.

After a few more days of rain, we loaded up and headed north, toward the swirling Red River, along with a steady stream of other crews. North Texas wheat farmers watched helplessly as we all drove away, leaving their fields to rot or eventually be cut for cattle feed. Our route to the river was a thin, shiny ribbon of wet asphalt stretching across a world of mud, rushing ditches, standing water, and ruined crops. Blame it on El Niño.

Here's how Andy Adams described the Red River at Doan's Crossing in *Log of a Cowboy*:

"...the majestic grandeur of the river was apparent on every hand, with its red waters marking the timber along its course, while the driftwood, lodged in trees and high on the banks, indicated what might be expected when she became sportive or angry. That she was merciless was evident, for although this crossing had been in use only a year or two when we forded, yet five graves, one of which was less that ten days made, attested her disregard for human life. It can safely be asserted that at this and lower crossings on Red River, the lives of more trail men were lost by drowning than on all other rivers together."

We made the crossing, a few miles downstream from Doan's, with no trouble. Our route over the next several weeks would be roughly parallel to the Great Western Trail, which ran north by northwest from the river through what is now Altus to Fort Supply, Dodge City, and Ogallala.

As we rose up out of the valley of the Red River we began to see patches of blue sky and bright patches of sunlight moving across the glittering plains. After we got past the town of Frederick the horizon became rumpled and dark ahead of us. We were coming up on the Wichita Mountains.

The Wichitas are an anomaly on the Southern Plains—the isolated granite remnant of an ancient, much larger mountain range. The body long ago melted, quite literally, into the surrounding plains. Only the hard granite backbone is left to face the wind and water, which are slowly but inevitably wearing it down, too. The boulders, house-size and larger, that lie against the range's core are rounded and smooth.

Out on the flat, open southern plains where everything is exposed to the bright light of the southern sun, and there are no secrets, the Wichitas promise respite, refuge, and mystery in their shady folds and dark, branching canyons. The steep hard slopes burst up from beneath the soil, up through the grass and the wheat, right up through the section line grid, and cast their irregular shadows across the land.

Deer, elk, bison, longhorn cattle, and other wildlife wander the secret interior valleys of the Wichitas unmolested. They step around old prospector digs, and over the long-erased campsites of Apache, Commanche, and Cheyenne hunting parties.

Custer and his Seventh Cavalry spent the winter of 1868-69 chasing the Cheyenne Chief Medicine Arrow and his ragtag band of refugees through and around the Wichitas, after the massacre at Black Kettle's village on the Washita River. The Indians had two white women with them as hostages.

Custer, with his own hostages in tow, finally caught up with Medicine Arrow and his family and followers on the open plains far west of the Wichitas. He rescued the white women and brought the refugees in to the reservation. The chase had lasted from November until March.

. . .

Mt. Scott is the highest and easternmost peak in the Wichita Mountains. It tops out at 2,467 feet. A modest height to be sure, but it counts for a lot out on the open plains. Since Mt. Scott is the eastern terminus of the range, the flat plains spread out to the far horizon north, east, and south of it. The horizon viewed from the top of Mt. Scott is so far away from you that even on the clearest days it is less a distinct line between the earth and sky, than it is a shimmery, liquid transformation from solid to gas.

We rolled north on Highway 183, past the Wichitas and the cloud shadows rippling over their flanks and the surrounding fields. The sky gradually opened up as we increased our distance from the Red River. We passed through Clinton, a Route 66 town. North of Clinton is a beautiful stretch of rolling wheat and ranch country.

Highway 183 was crowded with harvesters. As we drove

north we passed many other crews, in caravans like ours. The highway department has installed a pullout for harvest caravans and when we got to it we stopped for a quick lunch.

Just north of the South Canadian River crossing we passed through the town of Seiling. "Welcome Harvesters" read a sign at a convenience store. "Harvest Festival" read another sign at the implement dealer's store. A festival was indeed in progress. I picked up their local radio station, broadcasting a live remote from a booth at the festival. I heard mention of a rodeo scheduled for later that night.

We crossed the North Canadian, just out of Seiling, and then the Cimmaron River. After the Cimmaron crossing we drove past an area of sand dunes and into Waynoka, home of the annual Waynoka Rattlesnake Roundup.

From Waynoka it was a short trip on to Alva; home for Alan, Leota, Bill, and Jim.

We pulled into Alan's equipment yard and set up camp after a twenty-three-day false start south of the Red. Ripe wheat was all over the land in every direction.

We were in Alva about two weeks, and in that time we harvested about two thousand acres. The weather was often wet and stormy, the fields were almost always muddy, but the weather was far more cooperative than it had been south of the Red, and we took care of business.

was totally what it was in every detail.

It was pure,

essential,

undiluted.

On the Banks of the Salt Fork

The Salt Fork River flows down from the northwest and is deflected almost due east by high, rolling ground, about a hundred miles upstream from its confluence with the Arkansas River south of Ponca City. The Santa Fe Railroad crosses the Salt Fork at that sharp bend, and proceeds southwest. Where the railroad crosses the river, in the hollowed-out flood plain on the south bank, in the lee of the higher country to the west, sits the town of Alva. Alva is the county seat of Woods County. To the east the river cuts a straight line through level, fertile land for about thirty miles before it begins to meander southeast to its destination. This is wheat country. Wheat is virtually the only crop grown in Woods County, and many of the surrounding counties, too.

After we'd gotten settled into camp, I took my car out of the garage and drove south, back to Seiling, to the rodeo. I raced the setting sun and lost. About twenty miles from Seiling I picked up a live broadcast from the rodeo. I was delighted. I'd never before even considered the possibility of listening to a rodeo on the radio. The announcer was announcing for the crowd as well as for the radio. He kidded around with the rodeo clowns, and told us short, pithy stories about the broncs and bulls, and the young men attempting to ride them for money and small-town glory.

There was a cowboy from Australia.

"They're outta the chute, folks," the announcer said. "This young fella comes all the way from Australia. Imagine that, folks, all that way for—oops!—a six-second ride! How about a little applause, folks, for our wiry friend from down under. It was a good ride, it just wasn't long enough. Now next up we got a fella from out in Colorado, competin' for that fifteen-hunderd-dollar purse, folks!"

I heard a smattering of staticky applause, as I rolled south under a summer moon. My windows were down, there was no traffic, the road slipped past under my wheels, the stars filled the sky, and the wind blew through my hair.

There was a good crowd at the Harvest Days Rodeo. I slipped through the throngs of cowboys and cowgirls as inconspicuously as possible.

I dodged rambunctious little boys in hats and boots.

I discreetly stepped past young lovers turned inward.

I stood at the arena fence and watched the action. Middle-aged couples sat contentedly in the stands behind me. The glasses on the avid, transfixed faces of old men flickered reflections of the floodlit action in the arena before them.

I went around the line at the concession stand, and gave wide berth to the roving groups of local young cowboys.

I looked sideways at supple young women as they strolled by in impossibly tight jeans and silky blouses, trailing Lady Stetson in sweet counterpoint to the earthy, tangy smell of bullshit.

I soaked it all in.

It was a rodeo. It was totally what it was in every detail. It was pure, essential, undiluted.

I worked my way up close behind the chutes where the bulls and their riders met for their brief acquaintance.

The next morning dawned bright, clear, and calm. We got out to the field early, to grease and fuel the combines and tractor while we waited for the dew to dry from the wheat. We finished the service work in a few minutes and pulled the combines up to the header trailer and attached the headers. Then we sat down on the ground at the edge of the field to wait for the sun to do its work.

You can't harvest wheat if its moisture level is too high. One source of moisture in wheat is related to its level of ripeness. Another is from precipitation, including night dew squeezed out of the cooling, contracting air.

We lounged in the grass and made small talk while the morning sun dried the dew. Alan would know when it was time to try a round. "Richard, do you know how to tell if the wheat's dry of a morning?" Alan asked, lying back on one elbow, in the shade of his combine.

"How?"

"You listen to it. When it stops talkin' to you, it's ready. Listen."

I gazed out at the wheat and listened.

"Do you hear it cracklin'?"

I concentrated. "Yes, I do," I replied. A low, subtle, but unmistakable background crackle seemed to come from everywhere around us.

"That's the sound of the moisture leaving. When it stops, the moisture's all evaporated out and she's dry."

I nodded thoughtfully and continued to gaze out at the wheat. It followed the gentle dips and swells of the land out to the horizon, in unbroken purity in almost every direction. The wheat was yellow and the morning sky was blue, punctuated by little white clouds way up high, moving south. I took a deep breath through my nose.

Before too long, just as little beads of sweat began to appear on our foreheads, Alan gave the word and we fired up our machines. Alan swung his John Deere 9600 out into the field and cut a sufficient sample to test for moisture.

He got out of the cab and scooped a cup of grain from his bin, climbed down his ladder, and set his digital moisture tester on level ground. He poured the grain into the tester.

The tester is essentially a scale, about the size of a lunch box. You pour grain slowly into a receptacle until it reaches a sensor near the top, and a number comes up on the digital readout. That tells you that you've poured a specific volume of grain onto the scale. The tester is programmed to know how much a specific volume of grain weighs at a given moisture level. The less moisture, the less weight per volume. The tester weighs the grain, checks the weight against its database and, at the push of a button, gives you a LCD readout of the wheat's moisture content. Our goal was thirteen percent or less. The elevators don't like to take anything over that. It doesn't store well, for one thing.

We watched Alan kneel over his tester. I was in my tractor,

and Jim was in the other combine. Bill and Luke leaned against the front of the service truck. Their job was to drive the grain trucks into town to the elevator. Alan rose, climbed into his combine, and said over the radio, "Let's do it."

Jim fell into place behind Alan, cutting the next row, as they circled the field in a clockwise spiral toward the center. I slipped the tractor into gear and tagged along, pulling my grain cart over the stubble. I had my cab windows open and the pungent smell of fresh cut wheat filled the cab.

When Alan swung his auger out that was my signal that his bin was full. I pulled up beside him, centering my cart under his spout. He unloaded while we were on the move. My job was to set my tractor at a steady, comfortable speed and maintain a consistent distance to the left of the combine, so his spout remained over my cart. He adjusted his speed to match mine and when his spout was centered over the cart, he engaged his auger and unloaded, continuing to cut wheat the whole time. When his bin was empty, he swung his auger spout back in. That was my signal, along with a nod and a wave, and I arced out away from him, over the cut row and back down the row to fall in beside Jim and empty his bin in the same manner.

When they'd both unloaded into my cart, I drove back to the edge of the field to the grain trucks and unloaded into one of them.

How a Combine Works
(based on the John Deere 9600)

FIVE FUNCTIONS:

1. Cutting
2. Feeding
3. Threshing
4. Separating
5. Cleaning

CUTTING   Wheat is cut in the header assembly at the front of the combine. The header assembly includes the reel (that paddle wheel-like apparatus), the sickle, and an auger. The rotating reel pulls the wheat into the sickle which cuts the wheat and lays it on the feeder plate where the auger picks it up and delivers it into the feeder house.

FEEDING   The feeder house is the extension at the front of the combine to which the header is attached. Inside the feeder house is a conveyor which carries the cut wheat up into the cylinder-and-concave assembly for threshing.

THRESHING   The cylinder and concave work together to thresh the wheat, or remove the grains from the seed head. The cylinder pulls the wheat from the feeder house conveyor, and as it rotates, it pulls the wheat into tighter and tighter contact with a concave grate. The pressure and motion applied to the wheat between the rasp bars on the cylinder and the concave grate work together to grind the grain out of the seed head.

SEPARATING The grains, which are heavier than the chaff and straw, fall through the grate. This separates most of the wheat from the chaff and straw.

The chaff and straw are pulled by the cylinder further up over the concave grate and into contact with the beater. The beater, a rotating cylinder with paddles, pulls the chaff and straw away from the cylinder and concave, and delivers it to the straw walkers, which are a type of conveyor to carry the straw to the back of the combine, where it is dumped on the field.

CLEANING Meanwhile, the grains of wheat are delivered by augers to a system of screens in the airflow of a powerful fan, to further clean it. Then it's augered up to the bin on the top of the combine.

A feedback system captures loose grains that have been carried by the straw back to the straw walkers, and re-feeds the grains back into the cylinder and concave assembly. The straw walkers are designed to keep the straw agitated and suspended as they walk the straw to the back of the combine. This allows the grains to fall through the walkers and be captured for feedback.

When the bin is full the wheat is augered out into the back of a truck or other conveyance for delivery out of the field.

The John Deere 9600 is powered by a John Deere 7.6-liter, 260-horsepower, six-cylinder, turbo-charged, after-cooled diesel engine with a hydrostatic transmission.

The cabin is air-conditioned, heated, and pressurized to resist dust infiltration.

. . .

On a good day we could get an efficient rhythm going, so that the combines never stopped rolling.

One combine would fill and I'd be right there to unload it, finishing up just in time to circle back and catch the other combine as it filled.

Then, I'd hightail it back to the edge of the field, unload into a truck, and cut back across the field just in time to unload the combines again. We'd do this three times to fill one truck and send it to town, just as the other truck would come into view on its return from town.

Getting a good rhythm was what we strove for. We seldom achieved it that summer, though, because the fields were so often muddy. We spent a lot of time digging and pulling ourselves out of treacherous bogs, or probing and working our way around their irregular contours. This was time-consuming and hard on the equipment.

The John Deere 9600 is a fast, sophisticated machine, but ours was also a mechanical prima donna, subject to breakdowns.

Contending with the mud and breakdowns was also hard on

tempers, and Alan offered to fire me more than once during his frustrating summer, when he didn't feel I was pulling my weight.

On a good day, though, with the 9600 and the older 8820 both running well, on a dry, level field we could harvest thirty acres of wheat an hour. On days like that the hours would drone by as the combines spiraled toward the center of the fields, with hardly a word spoken among us over our two-way radios. Each of us did his part, lost in his own thoughts. When we finished a field, we moved to the next one and started over. When the weather and mechanical gremlins allowed, we continued into the night, sometimes until midnight, or until the night moisture began to seep into the wheat.

Then we'd drive the pickup back to camp in the dark, commenting on the day's work. After a short night's sleep we'd be up early the next morning for breakfast, and back to the fields to service and fuel the combines.

As we worked the wheat fields around Alva, we had to contend with frequent rain, but nothing like we'd suffered south of the Red River. The monsoon had continued unabated down there. We heard on the radio that the town of Vernon, Texas, received a twelve-inch rain one day not long after we'd left that country.

A few days later we heard that the water tower in Holliday had burst open and flooded the town with two hundred thousand gallons of water. Just what they needed.

On rainy days in Alva we worked in Alan's shop, doing busywork, trying to appear useful. Alan had us try to install an engine in his son's pickup. None of us had ever done it before, and it kept us busy as an ongoing project the whole time we were in Alva. We never did finish it.

On sunny days we worked long and late. One night, driving back to camp, Alan told me how his family had come to the area.

"My grandfather, who was from Kansas, came here in the land run of '93." (The land run of 1893 was one of several when that part of Indian Territory was first opened to white settlement and thousands of people lined up at the border, raced each other into the territory, and staked claims.) "He and a neighbor of his had come down together on horseback. When the signal was given they took off, and my grandfather found himself a quarter section he liked and dug him a hole in the ground and settled in. That was just a few miles south of where Alva is now. His friend found himself a quarter section nearby and settled in, too. My grandfather commenced to proving up on the land.

"His neighbor, though, got to missin' Kansas, so one day he come over to my grandfather's place and said he'd trade his quarter section to my grandfather for grandfather's horse, so he could get back to Kansas. I don't know what had happened to his own horse. Anyway, it was a good trade, so my grandfather traded with him, and found himself with a half section of land and no horse to leave on, so he knew he was here to stay.

"He did well. Before long he'd got himself a threshin' machine, which he pulled all over the county, threshin' wheat for the other farmers."

"So your grandfather was a custom harvester, too?"

"Yep. I come by it honestly. My dad hated the harvest, though. Wouldn't have a thing to do with it, so it skipped a generation. But now, between me and my brothers and our sons, there's seven of us out there custom harvestin', each runnin' our own crews."

"How long have you been doing it?" I asked.

"This is my thirty-fifth harvest," he replied. "I started out when I was about eighteen. It's about all I've ever done."

I was impressed. "So you've been traveling up and down the plains for thirty-five solid years, now, cutting wheat."

"That's right."

"You must know the Great Plains better than just about anybody. All the little towns, the back roads..."

"I know 'er pretty well, I guess. Leota, too. This is our thirty-fifth year of marriage."

"So you two have spent your whole lives together on the harvest."

"More or less."

It would be hard to imagine anyone who knows the Great Plains better, or who is better known on the Great Plains than Alan and Leota Nusser. I saw them greet and be greeted by people they knew in every town and camp we passed through. Sometimes people they hadn't seen in years would flag them down in a small town to say hello, and renew acquaintances.

Leota knows where to find what she needs to keep the camp going anywhere on the plains. And she knows what to take with her because it can't be found. She knows where all the Wal-Marts are and where they aren't.

Alan and Leota work hard, pay their bills on time, go to church, and honor their commitments. They take care of family.

They neither smoke nor drink, and seldom cuss.

They shake their heads in sad wonder at the luminescent world—sparkling and decadent—that washes up in the airwaves from the coasts and then drains back down. They've been to Vegas, and they've been to Hawaii, but they know where home is. They own a nice home in a nice neighborhood in a quintessential small town in the sunny middle of America, with a Lincoln in the garage and a Ford pickup in the driveway.

And yet they've lived a gypsy caravan life on two-lane roads, four to five months a year for the last thirty-five years. They've paid, fed, and worked shoulder to shoulder with a long stream of drifters, college boys, fugitives, farmboy-adventurers, immigrants, and refugees from the city. Living in a travel trailer, working the land, shopping the small towns, and meeting people from the Red River of the south to the Red River of the North and beyond.

They know where home is, all right. They could probably consider themselves a part of just about any community from Wichita Falls to Bismarck if they wanted. But Alva is where their roots are, as deep as roots get on the plains.

Alva, on the south bank of the Salt Fork of the Arkansas River, has a courthouse in a town square. It has an abandoned depot alongside the Santa Fe tracks. It has two thriving grain elevators, also along the tracks. It has an operating movie theater on the square. It has a diner. It has a western wear store. It has a college—Northwestern State College—covered in ivy beside U.S. Highway 64. It has a city park with a small zoo. It has neighborhoods with shady elms dappling the sunlight over well-trimmed shrubs and mowed lawns. It has convenience stores and motels along the highway. It has seedy bars on the edge of town. It has an airport. It has a Wal-Mart. It has bored teenagers roaming the streets on Saturday night. It has a local newspaper. It is surrounded on all sides by endless fields of wheat.

We squeezed every workable hour we could out of the time we had for the fields around Alva. So did every other harvest crew around. On dry, sunny days the fields were teeming with men and equipment. Look in any direction and you could see a half-dozen different crews busy between you and the horizon. A brown cloud of chaff and diesel exhaust hung low over the land. Sometimes the trucks took a long time getting back from the elevator, due to the long lines waiting to weigh in. Because my job kept me in the fields, I never got to see the lines of grain trucks waiting at the elevators, much to my regret.

One afternoon I had some free time, due to wet weather. I got in my car and drove west about thirty miles, to Freedom. Freedom sits on the north bank of the Cimmaron River, at a once-important cattle crossing. It's a small town. There is a city park at the east end of the main business street. In the park is a monument that the citizens have erected to honor the cattle barons who once ruled those parts, and the cowboys who worked for them. It has some of their biographies, complete with maps and portraits, all carved in granite, and set in a shelter. It's quite a monument. These men have not been forgotten by their grandchildren, or their grandchildren's children. Anyone who grows up around Freedom knows its story. It's written in the rock at the end of Main Street.

I sat in a thriving field of Indian Blankets atop a bluff on the south bank of the Cimmaron and watched the sun go slowly down.

A few days later we finished up around Alva and packed up and headed north. The magnetic North.

They've lived a gypsy caravan life on two lane r...

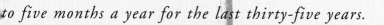

to five months a year for the last thirty-five years.

S*outh of the Smokey Hill River*

Bill took charge of getting the fleet ready to pull out. He was in a state of high excitement. He shouted orders and directed traffic, running from vehicle to vehicle, hitching up his pants with one hand and holding on to his hat with the other. He had us ready to go in no time at all.

We headed west to Buffalo, on U. S. 64. At Buffalo we turned right onto U. S. 183 north and began tacking northwest up onto one of the flattest parts of the Great Plains, northwest of Dodge City.

We stopped for lunch a few miles north of the Cimmaron River at the Sitka Social Club, in Sitka. Actually, the Sitka Social Club is Sitka. I had the best meal there that I had all summer. I had an omelet, which was a lot like one my wife might have made. The hash browns were fresh and crispy. The bread was home-baked whole wheat.

The Sitka Social Club is in a building that appears to have originally been a school, or depot, or Grange hall, or something.

In the foyer is a framed plat map of the planned town of Sitka. If any of it ever came to fruition, it has already ripened and withered, and the prairie has crept back over the old foundations. What's left is possibly the best restaurant on the Great

Plains, sitting by the tracks in stalwart isolation, surrounded by miles and miles of wheat fields and pastures, coyotes and jackrabbits, disregarded two-lanes and dusty stream beds. The smell of fresh bread hovers around the building like an aura.

After our meal we headed north a few miles and then west on 160 through Ashland. Somewhere near Ashland we crossed the wiped-away path of the Great Western Cattle Trail. Then north on 283, right up the one hundredth meridian, through the center of Big Basin. A few miles north of Big Basin we cut west to avoid Dodge City, and we were west of the one hundredth meridian for the first time.

We'd entered what must be the Ford Crown Victoria World Sales Capital. Every car we saw seemed to be a Crown Victoria.

We continued to tack north and west, crossing the Arkansas River at the town of Cimmaron. We went through Kalvesta and Dighton, and ended up at the Sokolosky farm eight miles north and eight miles east of Scott City. And twelve miles south of the Smoky Hill River.

The land in those parts, north of the Arkansas River, is surrealistically flat. It's so flat you can see as far sitting down on the ground as you can from atop your tractor. You can see everything from anywhere. If a farmer wants you to take your grain to a certain elevator, he merely has to point, though it may be twenty or thirty miles away.

Nature insists on being mysterious and will do what it must to remain so. On that flat plain she resorts to mirages. Though you can see everything, at a certain distance you get false information; things are distorted, shimmery, taller-looking than you know them to be, as if to rebel against the relentless horizontalness of the land. Evanescent lakes recede as you approach them.

We set up camp in the barnyard of a once fine horse ranch. Now the rancher's widow lives in town and the land is given over to the raising of wheat. The many outbuildings built to accommodate thoroughbred horses sit idle and spotless around the house, where Lee Steinmetz and his wife live and manage the farm. They had two thousand acres for us to harvest. We would fight deep, tractor-swallowing mud for virtually every acre.

Once we set up our camp in the barnyard, Leota called us on the intercom from her trailer to ours to tell us that supper was ready. We filed across the yard and lined up at her door. Silent Jim was in a good mood. On the way over he slipped up behind me and got me in a headlock, much to my surprise. I quickly reversed it on him and we broke apart, grinning. Then it was over. We'd barely broken stride. Leota leaned out her door and handed down our dinners, with her ever-present smile.

We were all grateful for Leota that summer, so far from our wives and mothers. Not only for her home-cooked meals, but for her femininity, which was a civilizing influence. At breakfast she would come to her door to dole out our eggs (fried beyond belief) and Tang, barefoot, wrapped tightly in her robe, smiling down at us as we lined up in the dewy grass. She handed down our plates with a pleasant word or two for everyone.

As we finished our supper, I asked Luke why he'd come on the harvest.

"Well, I've known guys that have done it, and it's always

sounded like a good time. Besides, my wife and me figured if I got out of Missouri for a while it might keep me out of trouble. And I can save some money, maybe. What are you doing here?" he asked me.

I should have expected the question. I'd brought up the subject. Still, it caught me off guard. After a moment, I shrugged. "I dunno," I said.

Jim tapped the cards loudly on the table. Luke and I looked at him.

He smiled. "Let's play cards."

We cleared off the table and got out our coffee cans of change.

"Three of a kind beat two pair?" Jim asked after the first deal. None of us could keep that straight, for some reason.

We agreed to say yes and play it that way.

"So, Jim, why are you here?" I asked a few minutes later.

Jim studied his cards, sucking air through the hole where his front tooth once was. "I dunno," he shrugged after a while. "It's a job. I done it before. Gimme two."

I gave him two cards, and Luke one. I took two also.

Bill, who wasn't playing, put on a tape of Red Sovine's greatest hits.

Outside the window, the moon rose over the barn, over the fields, over the earth.

"You going to work for Alan after the harvest or look for something else?" I asked Jim.

He shrugged. "I dunno. Hadn't really thought about it, yet." He squinted at his cards. "Flush beat a full house?" he asked.

"No. I fold."

"Me too," said Luke. We threw in our cards and Jim raked in the meager pot.

"What about you, Bill?" I asked him.

Bill, who had been singing along quietly with the tape and absentmindedly watching our game, was shaken from his reverie by the sound of his name. "What?" he asked.

"How come you're working the harvest? You got a pension from the Air Force and a wife at home. How come you're sitting in this tin shack with the likes of us?"

"I don't know," he replied. "It's something to do. I just like it. I don't know." He lapsed back into his reverie.

After night had fallen I walked out past the barnyard to the edge of the wheat that surrounded the house and its cluster of outbuildings. I leaned on the fence and looked out at the glistening wheat waving in the moonlight. I stood there for about the time it would take to slow smoke a cigarette, if I smoked, and pondered my motives. What was I doing there?

I listened to the wheat whisper in the cool night breeze. If there was an answer contained in that dry whisper that rose all around me, it was coming from too many places at once, and too softly. I couldn't quite make it out.

The next day we cut wheat. The field was dry and level. We averaged almost thirty acres per hour. That was the best day we had. Most of the rest of our work was hampered by mud. If a field had muddy areas we'd probe their perimeters, working in as close as we could, and come back to it after a couple of dry days to finish it out. Sometimes we'd have to come back a second time, even though we might have worked our way to another field miles away. I got my tractor stuck a couple of times, and the combines got stuck numerous times, since they did the probing. When a combine got stuck, the other one would have to come over to it and pull it out. We left a lot of trenches in the fields that stormy summer.

Once a tornado passed by about fifteen miles from us. I went outside to see it, which would have been easy in that open country, but a wall of rain obscured the funnel.

I remember one evening the most intense, prolonged lightning storm I've ever witnessed. It came out of the west, and for four hours it grew and crept over the plains toward us, keeping the sky constantly lit as the sun went down behind it. Luke stood on the top of his grain truck and watched it bear down on our field.

He stood up there like a lightning rod, facing the wind, grinning with the exhilaration of youth, and convinced of his immortality. I fussed at him until he finally came down.

Jim, Alan, and I made our rounds with a growing sense of urgency as the storm bore down on us with terrible slowness, and the last round of wheat drew ever closer. It was a race, a contest of nerves between Alan and God. Alan won, though I suspect God let him win. We got the last load out of the field and in a truck, under a tarp, just as the first giant raindrops began to splatter down. The lightning by then was no longer just out of the west, but all over the night sky. We drove home in the rain, in high spirits, all agreeing that it had been a magnificent show.

The next day we were off duty, so we drove over to Scott City. I searched all over town for a bookstore—new, used, or otherwise—but in vain. Scott City is a good-sized town, a county seat. Someone could do well to open a bookstore there. There was a bestseller rack at the grocery store, but, desperate as I was for something to read, I couldn't raise an interest in anything I saw there.

I went to the public library, but of course couldn't check anything out. Luke went in with me, but he only stayed for a minute. I browsed their local history section for anything on the old cattle trails. I discovered that the Great Western trail had passed north out of Dodge City a good ways east of us.

When I went back outside, Luke, Jim, and Bill were lounging under a tree on the library lawn. Jim had gotten a haircut.

As we walked to the truck, Luke asked me how much it cost to check out a book from the library.

I was as surprised by his question as he was by my answer. "Well, nothing, Luke," I said. "It's free." I looked at him quizzically.

"Nothing?" he seemed genuinely shocked to learn this. "Then how do they make their money?"

"They don't make money, they just lend out books."

"Well, they have to make money, they have bills to pay," Luke insisted.

I explained the concept of public libraries to Luke. He'd never been in one, until that day, because he'd always assumed it would cost him money, and no one had ever told him otherwise.

On the way back to camp I made Bill take us on a side trip

to El Cuartelejo. El Cuartelejo is a ruin, the site of the east-ernmost known Pueblo. A stream flowing north into the Smoky Hill River has carved a scenic canyon out of the plains, and the modest ruin is situated at an especially pretty bend in that stream. It's believed to have been built by Indians who'd fled the Spanish invaders in what is now New Mexico. They seem to have had a refined sense of aesthetics, judging from the pretty site they picked to build their house.

From El Cuartelejo we drove north to the edge of the Smoky Hill River valley, ("the Smoky Hill River valley"—what a pleasant mouthful!), then east along its rounded shoulder. When we were due north of our camp, we drove down into the valley and crossed a stream at the bottom. On the north bank we crossed the trace of the old Butterfield Stage route. We didn't realize that we'd crossed the Smoky Hill River at first, because its valley is at least five miles across, and a couple hundred feet lower than the plain, but the stream that wallowed out that valley is narrow enough to jump across, and about knee deep. After we'd seen the "river" and its valley, we drove straight south twelve miles to our camp for a long, relaxing evening.

I developed a habit of rising at dawn and putting on a pot of coffee while my compadres slept. I'd slip out the door and walk around the yard with a cup of coffee as the birds and barnyard cats woke up. After a short walk I'd sit in Lee's immaculate workshop, sipping coffee and listening to country music on his radio. I never got over how neat and clean his workshop was. Since they stopped raising horses, there's just not that much for Lee to do, most of the year, so his tools stay put, and his floors stay clean.

Slowly, with the gathering light, the camp would come alive, for breakfast and another day's work.

Our last day there we worked a field that went right up to the curved rim of the Smoky Hill River valley. Luke, Bill, and I stopped our vehicles at the edge of the field. Alan and Jim had preceded us and were already plying their way through the wheat. As we stood in the shade of one of the trucks I looked down and saw a snake about three feet from me, slipping furtively away in the stubble.

"Hey, look, a snake!" I moved in for a closer look.

Luke and Bill gathered around and we began to try to identify it.

The snake was keeping a low profile. It seemed to want to leave the scene with as little fuss as possible. We, however, were intensely curious about it. I leaned over it for a close look.

"What is it?" I mused.

"A rat snake?" Luke conjectured.

"Maybe a corn snake?" offered Bill.

I looked at its head. It had the shape of a poisonous snake. I stepped back a little. "What about a copperhead?" I asked, even though the color wasn't right, and it was larger than the ones I'd seen around Tulsa. This one appeared to be a little under three feet long.

Luke, who was from the Ozarks, had seen a lot of copperheads. "Might be," he conceded doubtfully. "You better get back, if it is. They'll bite you. They're poison."

The snake, which had shown no sign of aggressiveness, had slowly sidled away from us, looking for shelter from our burning gazes. I leaned over it again and looked at its tail closely for the first time. I leapt back.

"Hey!" I shouted. "Are those rattles?"

Sure enough they were. And to prove it, the snake shook them weakly at me.

We all gave the snake some room, and looked it over with new respect. Its behavior was so uncharacteristic of the few rattlers I'd encountered, it hadn't seemed possible for it to be one. The timber rattlers I'd come across in eastern Oklahoma were aggressive and willing to stand their ground. They'd rattle their tails at you vigorously, leaving no room for mistaken identity.

This snake, however, was so shy and retiring, we'd all been fooled. The reason, we discovered upon careful examination, was that we'd apparently run over his tail with one of the trucks. This had robbed him of his warning apparatus, making him all the more dangerous. Fortunately, he seemed to be in a state of shock from the injury, and was slow and weak. Only when I had really leaned in close had he been roused to a sufficient panic to force his tail up and shake it at me.

Bill went to the service truck and brought back a pipe about five feet long and pinched the rattler's head off. Then he buried the head.

We never discussed or even thought about whether or not to kill the snake. It was a reaction, not a decision. Each of us heard the same voice from the same hidden chambers deep in

our brains, a common ancestor hissing, "Kill it! Kill it now!"
We heard and we obeyed.

After Bill had buried the snake's head, he placed the body,
his trophy, in the back of the service truck, and we got on with
our day's work. We were about thirty miles from the elevator
so I had a considerable amount of wait time for the trucks to
return. During that time I would sit on top of the grain in the
cart hitched to my tractor and enjoy the view. It was an intensely sunny day.

The view south over the flat land was astonishing to me. I
could watch Luke's truck coming back from the elevator for a
full fifteen minutes before it arrived. The landscape south was
punctuated near and far with the ubiquitous elevators, vertical
concrete tubes shimmering in the distance.

The view north was different and just as striking. We were
at the wavy line where the flat, intensely cultivated plain that
stretches up all the way from the Arkansas River in the south
gives way to the broad valley of the Smoky Hill River.

The wheat field gave way to a pasture that is fractured by
a canyon that winds down into the main valley. The sides of
the graceful, broad valley slope gently down to the ancient
riverbed. It is miles across and virtually treeless, except along
the slender, meandering watercourse in the basin. The many
side washes give pleasing shape, texture, and shade to the grassy
valley sides. The far horizon fades to a pale smoky blue.

We finished up just before sunset. As the rest of the crew
drove back to camp, I lingered for a while just to be alone and
quiet in a beautiful spot. I sat on top of my tractor cab and

silently witnessed the effortless wheeling of day into night. It was a sunset without histrionics. No high-voltage hum, no grinding gears, no hydraulic hiss. Whoever was in charge had obviously done it before.

A thin crescent moon fell slowly through the sky, like a fingernail clipping falling to the bottom of the sea.

The stars came out slowly at first, and then more quickly.

I awoke early from the deep,

dreamless sleep of a hard-working man

ar conscience,

nd stepped outside into the early morning light.

$\mathcal{T}$*he   Frenchman   River   Valley*

The next day was Saturday, July fourth, our fifty-first day in the field. We broke camp right after breakfast.

Bill, for obscure reasons of his own, tried to give the rattlesnake carcass to the Steinmetz's, but they steadfastly refused to accept it.

"No, thank you, Bill," Lee said. The headless snake lay stretched out on the barnyard gravel between them. Lee's dog barked at it from a safe distance. Lee's wife went in the house. "You just take that snake with you to Nebraska, or ever where you're goin'."

By 10:40 we were rolling. Alan took the lead as usual, and Bill brought up the rear after letting us get a few minutes head start.

We headed west to Highway 83 and turned north to join the flow of other harvest caravans. We stopped at Oakley where Alan had arranged to meet our last customer and get paid. While Alan and Leota took care of business, the rest of us walked up the street to Pizza Hut for lunch. When we returned we saw Alan talking to a highway patrolman. It turned out that Bill had unwittingly veered left into a pickup pulling a stock trailer as it had tried to pass him. Neither the woman driving the pickup nor the horse in the trailer were hurt. Bill, driving the semi-tractor and pulling a combine, hadn't even felt it. He was shocked when he was informed of the accident. When he was shown the scrape marks on the combine tires he began to curse himself. Alan, wearing a stormy expression, didn't bother to disagree with Bill's low self-appraisals.

There were statements to make, forms to fill out, records to check, and a phone call to make. Then we were on our way again.

Between Oakley and Colby we crossed the north and south forks of the Solomon River, and the Saline River. At Colby we turned north on Highway 25.

We crossed the Republican River at the Trenton Dam. As Alan pulled off the dam I heard him ask Leota over the radio if she thought he should turn left at the upcoming intersection.

"Nusser," she shot back, "if you do, I'll stomp a mud hole in you!"

I hadn't heard that phrase before and was quite amused. Leota told me later that Alan had been teasing her, because, two years earlier he had for some reason turned left at that intersection and they'd followed him and he'd gotten stuck on a bridge with his wide load. They'd had to back up a quarter of a mile and had caused a severe traffic tie-up.

We turned right onto Highway 34 for a few miles and drove past a historical marker denoting the old Texas Cattle Trail, which had crossed the Republican River at or near the damsite.

I didn't have a chance to stop and read the marker, being in convoy, but Andy Adams had described this crossing of the Republican River in *Log of a Cowboy*. When his cowboys had crossed the river there was a tent set up a couple of miles downstream.

The cowboys were given a word of advice about the tent from a man who knew:

"There's a deadfall down here on the river," said he, "that robs a man going and coming. They've got booze to sell you that would make a pet rabbit fight a wolf. And if you can't stand the whiskey, why, they have skin games running to fleece you as fast as you can get your money to the centre. Be sure, lads, and let both their whiskey and cards alone.'"

They didn't, and before the night was over they had, almost to a man, found themselves stripped of their guns, saddles, and cash due to a crooked horse race that had looked like a sure thing.

Their boss was so amused at their plight when they returned to camp, abashed and forlorn, that he advanced them enough pay to buy back their saddles and guns, so they could get on up the trail.

We followed 25 up to Highway 6 which we followed northwest up the Frenchman River Valley to the town of Wauneta. This is a pretty, fertile valley, planted more in corn than wheat. The corn was all in pitiful shape, stunted and yellow. This was due, we later found out, to a spring drought followed by a late freeze—May twenty-fifth. These same conditions had also pretty much ruined the wheat planted up on the surrounding plains.

Our arrival in Wauneta was well noted. We pulled into the city-owned RV park, joining some other harvesters, and within minutes the town marshall had come by to turn on the water and power for us. A few minutes after the marshall had left, a city worker arrived to make sure that the utilities had been turned on. Right after the city worker, Alan's customer arrived to say hello to Alan and go over some details of the job.

We set up camp under some big cottonwood trees, and Alan took us all downtown to the Sailor Inn for supper. It was Saturday night and the special was prime rib. We all had some. Mine was a trifle well done but still a treat.

After supper I took a walking tour of the pretty, self-contained town of Wauneta, nestled in the valley of the Frenchman River. I finished my walk by climbing up out of the valley for an overview. The river upstream cuts a gorge through the sandy, grass-covered plains, and as it washes down toward the Republican River at Culbertson, the gorge widens out into a valley. A complex system of picturesque canyons and arroyos finger out from the main channel, cutting into the pastures and wheat fields up on the tableland.

A serious-looking storm was chugging in from the northwest. I raced it back to camp.

That humid, stormy evening we heard on the radio that a tornado had passed not far east of our Smoky Hill River camp after we'd left.

We started to work for Mr. Clyde Hoff Sunday morning, north of town, up out of the valley. Alan told me he considers him one of the best farmers he's ever known. He's a long-time resident of the area, so I asked him about the Texas-Ogallala Cattle Trail. He told me that you could still see its trace at its crossing of the Frenchman, downstream at the village of Hamlet. I made up my mind to ask Alan if I could drive down the valley to see the trace if the opportunity presented itself.

We finished our work for Mr. Hoff Monday evening. His crop had suffered badly from the drought and freeze, but not as badly as the farmers south of the river. He'd gotten twenty to twenty-five bushels per acre.

Since we'd arrived Saturday several other harvest crews had joined us at camp. Alan and Leota knew them all. A crew run by a woman parked next to us. One of their crew members told me one evening that their farmers were south of the river. They'd cut about a hundred acres for one unlucky farmer and gotten only about three bushels per acre.

Apparently the freeze had occurred at a vulnerable time in the wheat's development and killed the seed head. So there were tens of thousands of acres of wheat in an area roughly bounded the Platte and Smoky Hill Rivers, waving in the summer winds with virtually no grain in the heads. It was a disaster. Word was that farther north, north of the sandhills, the wheat had been in such an early stage of development that it hadn't been as seriously affected by the freeze.

We heard through the grapevine that farmers south of the Red River were offering upwards of twenty dollars an acre for any harvesters that would turn around and head south and try to help them save their crop. There were few takers.

The next day we worked till nearly midnight. All afternoon huge, magnificent thunderheads ballooned up east of us and rolled further east, wreaking violent havoc on the farms and towns over that way. For us, it was a pleasant, sunny day. I watched the clouds form and march off as I worked.

I listened to an AM station out of McCook, and the country music was frequently interrupted by lengthy weather bulletins read by a young lady in a halting, endearing, little-girl voice. She warned us all about the dangers of lightning, in the manner of a baby-sitter telling toddlers about light sockets.

Hail the size of lemon drops was slicing through what remained of the corn crop in Red Willow County, she informed us. She'd cut off Clint Black in mid-verse. She told us to stay tuned, stay calm, and stay away from windows.

I loved the sound of her little-girl voice bravely pushing its way through the storm-tossed airwaves, reading, misreading, and rereading the latest crucial information to us, her voice submerged momentarily by thunderous static on our AM receivers, then bobbing determinedly to the surface again to continue her report.

Meanwhile, the thunderheads continued to spawn and grow in the eastern sky, while we worked under the warm sun.

We worked our way wordlessly through the fields, each

in his own machine, listening to his own radio, lost in his own thoughts.

I got to thinking about the minute hands on clocks. I can't see them move on a typical indoor clock, but that's a function of the clocks' radius. The bigger the radius, the faster the hand has to move to sweep out a circle in an hour. At exactly what radius, I wondered, does that motion become detectable? Is it different for different people, or is there a General Threshold Radius for us all?

When we finally quit that night, we'd brought in over three hundred acres, our best day yet. The half moon shone brightly in the star-filled sky, throwing our shadows across the stubble as we walked wearily to the truck for the drive back to camp.

The next morning, I awoke early from the deep, dreamless sleep of a hard-working man with a clear conscience, and stepped outside into the early morning light.

The morning breeze was fresh and sweet, winnowing up the Frenchman Valley, billowing Wauneta's curtains to let the sun shine in her open windows. The sunrise was a brilliant yet tasteful arrangement in blues, rosy pinks, and pale yellows. The harvest camp was quiet. I sat in a lawn chair and sipped a cup of coffee.

Before long Leota had roused my compadres and served us a simple breakfast of microwaved sweet rolls, chewy bacon, and chilled Tang. The rest of the guys ate in the trailer. I scooted my lawn chair over to the back of the service truck and used its back bumper as a table.

The harvest camp came to life as I sat there thoughtfully chewing my bacon.

Doors opened and closed. Figures emerged into the light. Low voices and quiet laughter.

I sipped my coffee and Tang.

Somebody rummaged through a toolbox down the line. A blue jay became upset and left the camp, complaining loudly.

I tried hard to memorize everything, every bit of just one moment, though now I remember next to nothing, except the desire to remember.

Suddenly I was in the middle of something like a fire drill. My compadres came tumbling out of the trailer in a hell of a hurry, grabbing lunch buckets, swarming around me and hollering "Come on! Let's go to work!" Luke leaped up onto the back of the service truck to get his water jug, nearly spilling my morning coffee. Jim had jumped into the service truck cab and fired up the engine. He appeared ready to back over me.

Alan stood in the middle of the uproar smiling benignly. The morning sun reflected brightly off his glasses, hiding his eyes.

I wolfed down my roll, dumped out my Tang, grabbed my coffee cup and stalked angrily into the trailer to brush my teeth.

I care about my teeth.

I rode with Jim to the field in the service truck. We were the first ones to arrive. I was cranky and sullen all the way, but when we arrived I found it impossible to maintain my indignation on such an overwhelmingly beautiful country morning.

The sky was such a hard enamel blue you could almost hear it ringing over the rippling yellow wheat. There was no dew that morning, so Jim and I set about greasing, fueling and cleaning the combines right away. When Alan arrived, we would be ready to cut wheat.

After we'd gotten the combines ready, we had a few minutes before the rest of the guys arrived. I watched a Swainson's Hawk search for an early-morning thermal over the wheat.

Swainson's were the most common hawk I saw that summer. They are drawn to the combines, which expose their prey and get it moving. They hover high over the field, pacing the combines, and when they spot a mouse or ground squirrel scurrying through the stubble they fold their wings and hurl themselves to the earth in a thrilling, breathtaking dive. A few feet above the ground they abruptly check their dive, make a final adjustment in their trajectory, and then pounce.

When we finished that day our work was done in the Frenchman Valley. Though we stayed in that valley only a week, due to the failed crop, I remember it more vividly than any other place we stayed that summer. I'd like to go back someday and follow the Frenchman River further upstream.

I got up at seven the next morning and my stirring aroused Bill who trudged past me in the trailer, in an endorphin daze. I dressed quickly and walked downtown to the Sailor Inn for breakfast. I was their only customer.

Later, Alan ducked his head in the trailer door and told us he and Leota were going golfing. "You all can wash trucks, watch TV, sit on your butts, or whatever you want," he said.

I saw my chance. "Would you mind if I drove down to Hamlet and took a look at the old cattle trail?" I asked.

"You can do that," Alan said kindly.

And so I did. After I disentangled myself from Hamlet's postmistress, who told me much more than I'd realized I'd wanted to know about Hamlet (formerly Hudson), I followed her directions to the top of the south slope of Frenchman Valley, on Stratton Road. The road joined the old trail as it approached the valley from the south. Looking down into the valley I could see the trace of an older, long-abandoned roadway veering off to the west and down to the valley floor.

Hudson, the postmistress had told me, had been a way station on a stage line that had run up the valley. Cowboys had used Hudson as a place to send and receive mail.

I carefully studied the old trace descending into the valley and searched the north slope for signs of its ascent back up to the plain. After a minute, even in the flat light of midday, I saw what I was looking for. A low hillock a little ways up from the valley floor had an unnatural notch worn out of it, made by more than two million hooves that had trudged up that slope. Further up the slope, and to the right, next to a wheat field, I could see the wide trace curve on up out of the valley. The difference between the trace and the surrounding land was subtle, but, once you saw it, unmistakable. It was a different shade of green, and seemed to have less Yucca growing in it.

I savored the view and imagined Andy Adams' cowboys looking over the same view from their mounts as they herded thirty thousand head of longhorns down the slope to the crossing. This was their last water hole before Ogallala.

We spent the remainder of the day getting the camp and equipment ready to travel.

After supper, as the sun lowered itself toward the horizon, I took a walk out of Wauneta up the valley's south slope. I sat on the rim of a side canyon with the sun to my back.

I sat as still as the canyon itself and slipped into a trance, mesmerized by the shadow of the canyon's west wall creeping along the canyon floor, and up the east wall. I could actually see it move. A doe appeared on the opposite side of the canyon and stared fixedly at me. I stared back, wondering if I could outlast her. We remained immobilized, gazing at each other for a solid half hour. It was "deeply meaningless," to borrow a phrase from Jim Harrison.

The light grew dim. Over in town a little league game was in full swing. The cheers and squeals of the crowd reverberated through all the side canyons, the arroyos, the washes, up and down the valley. A coyote not far from me began to answer their cries. After a while the ball game ended.

A hard, bright half-moon sailed through the sky above us all. I pictured its light pouring through my bedroom window in Tulsa, across my wife's sleeping face.

...early impossible to estimate.

$\mathcal{A}$cross the Missouri River

The next day was our longest travel day yet. Our trail parted from that of Andy Adams' cowboys. We got up before dawn and were on the road by 6:30. We took Highway 25 north to Sutherland and followed U. S. 30 east down the Platte River valley to the town of North Platte, at the confluence of the North and South Platte Rivers. We headed north out of North Platte on U. S. 83 up out of the Platte River valley and across the eastern Sandhills. We crossed the South Loup, the Middle Loup, the Dismal, and the North Loup Rivers.

The Sandhills, I noted with approval, were just as I'd left them a year earlier. We crossed the Niobrara and took a short break in Valentine. North of Valentine we drove through the Rosebud Indian Reservation to the town of Mission.

The land from Mission north to Pierre is uniquely beautiful. The rolling hills are covered with wild clover. The clover was a deep, rich green, over-sprayed with small yellow blossoms stretching from horizon to horizon in an unbroken expanse. There is a visual purity to that landscape that's difficult to convey. Virtually no trees, houses, wires, fences, or roads mar the visual impact.

The whole world smells like honey up there. There can't be any place else like it on earth.

And then there's Murdo, named for Murdo McKenzie, legendary cattle baron. Murdo spreads out from Interstate 90 like a pox upon that beautiful land, a colorful monument to tacky roadside capitalism erected on a thin bed of asphalt, smelling of diesel and grimy dollars. There are plenty of places like it.

We crossed the mighty Missouri River at Pierre, which, as every sixth-grader knows, is the capital of South Dakota. It was rush hour, but rush hour in Pierre is not that big of a deal. The population is around thirteen thousand.

The Missouri River in that country forms a boundary between two topographies. The river is like a rope trying to hold back the West, to contain it, to keep it west of the one hundredth meridian.

The country west of the Missouri in South Dakota is characterized by rolling, grass-covered hills, sparse, meandering roads, and fast-flowing rivers washing down from the Black Hills and the eastern foothills of the Northern Rockies. The rivers—the White, the Bad, the Cheyenne, the Moreau, and the Grand—all feed into the west bank of the Missouri. These rivers flow through the Fort Pierre, Buffalo Gap, and Grand River National Grasslands. It is Indian Country, containing the Standing Rock, Cheyenne River, Rosebud, Brule, and Pine Ridge Reservations.

The country east of the Missouri is flat—really flat—almost as if a giant ice sheet, maybe thousands of feet thick, had once ground its way out of the north over the land, and then slowly receded as it melted away, leaving the scoured, featureless plain in its wake. That country today is intensely cultivated, and devoid of significant streams between the Missouri and the James Rivers. East of the James, the Big Sioux flows south into the Missouri's east bank at Sioux City. The James feeds into the Missouri at Yankton and is the last significant tributary to feed the Missouri from its east bank for many hundreds of miles. The road system lies over that flat, captured land like a net.

Gettysburg was our destination, an isolated town of about sixteen hundred people surrounded by farmland, east of the Missouri River. It is about sixty miles north-northeast of Pierre, sitting astraddle of the one hundredth meridian.

We arrived at Gettysburg about 7:00 p.m. Alan had been up since midnight, unable to sleep, and then led our convoy on a day-long journey of about four hundred miles north, pulling wide loads. He was tired, and a little cranky. While we were setting up camp in our lot in town, there was a problem finding an adapter plug for the electrical pole.

"I gave it to you!" Bill assured Alan with wide blue eyes.

"That's a load of bull crap!" Alan shot back fiercely, which turned out to be more or less true when we found it a few minutes later.

After we'd gotten set up Alan took us out to dinner, and, because he's a decent man, roused himself from his state of fatigue and ire to regale us all with stories during supper.

I particularly remember him telling us about a beekeeper he'd once met who follows the blossoming flowers from Texas to South Dakota every year with his bees. I didn't pay much attention to the conversation after that.

The next day was chilly, damp, gray, and heavy.

We found out that the wheat we were there to cut wouldn't be ready for at least a week and a half. We were ahead of schedule because of the failed crop around Wauneta.

I looked at the clay-colored clouds rolling in from the northwest with dread, remembering the awful tedium we'd suffered in Holliday. Here the tedium of sitting in a trailer in the rain with three other guys, whom I already knew too well, would be magnified by the isolated location of Gettysburg. Even if the sky did clear, the wheat wasn't ready.

I became depressed. I thought about Alan, and how he'd picked one thing, early in life, and stuck with it. It seemed I had spent my life getting off on wrong floors, and waiting in lobbies for the elevator to come back around.

I took a walk around town, under brooding skies. I visited a new museum, the Dakota Sunset Museum. I could smell fresh paint when I walked in. The Dakota Sunset Museum had been built primarily, it seems, to protect and display the Medicine Rock.

The Medicine Rock is a rock approximately ten by five by three feet in size. This rock was once situated near the east bank of the Missouri River, and was considered sacred by the Sioux Indians. It was sacred because it has two human footprints and a hand print embedded deeply in its surface. The Sioux considered these prints proof of the existence of God, I'm told. The

Sioux often left offerings at the rock. The rock was well known in the nineteenth century. In her book *Boots and Saddles*, Elizabeth Custer mentioned passing by it on her journey with her husband up the Missouri.

When Lake Oahe was built, flooding the Missouri, the rock was moved to Gettysburg. Specifically, it ended up in the lot of a restaurant at the east end of town. The restaurant changed its name to the Medicine Rock Cafe. The rock sat there for several years. People liked to carve their initials in its surface, and this became a growing concern.

This mysterious rock was an important part of the region's history, and it needed to be protected. The desire to protect this rock made the citizens of Gettysburg realize that they needed a museum. Not only for the rock, but for the mementos of their own short but growing history in the area.

So they built the Dakota Sunset Museum. A smattering of other exhibits have already been placed on display, including a history of the town in snapshots, and—my favorite—an extensive pen and pencil collection displayed in custom-made glass cases.

The centerpiece of the museum, however, the rock, is sitting alone—silent, still, inscrutable—in its own climate-controlled, track-lighted room, just off the building's main entrance. Its room has a picture window facing the street so we may view the rock when the museum is closed.

It is a mystery, isn't it? Who made those footprints, and that handprint? The footprints are seven feet apart, and buried deep in what must have been soft clay at the time. How long ago was it?

The museum is minded by an elderly lady who suggested to me that the handprint could have been made by someone pushing himself up from the soft earth. The footprints, being so far apart, seemed to her to be the prints of someone fleeing in terror.

Perhaps, she suggested, from a grizzly bear. Grizzlies were once common in the area, she assured me. As evidence of her grizzly bear scenario, she showed me some other deep impressions in the rock that could have been grizzly bear prints, though they were admittedly rather vague.

"Grizzly," she said.

I believe it. I also believe the Medicine Rock is still sacred, in a way, sacred now to white people. Parts of its surface, reachable from across the cordon that surrounds it, are shiny, polished with oil from the hands of those who have come to the Dakota Sunset Museum to ponder its mystery, and felt compelled to reach across and touch it. I touched it.

The rock and the museum built to accommodate it cheered me up temporarily, but by evening the leaden, blustery skies had driven me into the Firehouse Tavern for a shot and a beer, in open violation of my pledge to Alan. I glanced guiltily over my shoulder as I went in. The Firehouse shares the building with the real firehouse, the one with fire trucks and a tower with a siren. The tavern was dark. It has no windows and is mainly lit by numerous hanging lights, the shades of which all advertise Grain Belt Beer.

A thick Saturday night crowd clinked glasses and smacked pool balls. They blew clouds of smoke and gestured enthusiastically. They played the jukebox, and watched the game on television. They laughed and cursed too loudly. They spilled beer on the tables and flicked ashes on the floor. They were having a good time.

I sat down hopefully at the bar and ordered a shot of Irish whiskey and a glass of Grain Belt. They had neither, so I had a glass of whatever they had on tap and a shot of Jack Daniels. I was bored. I tried to soak up the ambiance, but it rolled off me like water off a duck. I glanced up at the baseball game on the television above the bar and said something about it to the man sitting next to me. He agreed with whatever it was I'd said, drank up, paid his tab, and left the building. I became morose.

I walked back to camp, dodging mud puddles and resisting the impulse to call my wife. I'd decided early in the summer to only call her when I was in a good mood.

. . .

The days and nights groaned slowly by in sullen resistance to the persistent northwest wind. We sat in the trailer and played cards, mostly solitaire, and watched the Olympics on TV.

One night Luke, Jim, and I got ridiculously drunk at the Firehouse while Alan and Leota were in North Dakota, looking over the crop and lining up business. We hogged the pool table, playing atrociously. I was bad, and got worse as the night progressed, but Luke was terrible right from the start and stayed that way. Jim quietly kicked our butts time and again. We had a good time, and before we knew it we were being invited to leave so the bartender could go home. We discovered that three drunken men can't sneak through a tin trailer in the middle of the night without waking a sleeping sober one, no matter how hard they try.

The next day was a day of misery. I squinted into the bright, hard sunshine like a lost miner. I'd been sober so long I'd forgotten about hangovers. Suitable penance, I told myself, for breaking my now trampled vow not to drink. Luke, with youth on his side, woke up miserable, but bounced back to life after breakfast. Jim was as stoic as a cow in the rain. I kept my head down and tried to take my punishment like a man. Bill was amused.

I was pretty much recovered by the time Alan and Leota returned from the north about 5:30. Just before sunset a storm blew in from west of town. It was a marvelous sight. The rain was falling from roiling clouds in billowing curtains, back-lit by the setting sun. The storm bore down on us swiftly and I went outside to watch. I could hear a constant, low roar from the storm, the likes of which I'd never heard before. It grew louder every second.

"Hey, listen," I called to the guys in the trailer, "It's roaring!"

Alan overheard me from his trailer. "Roaring?" he asked through his window.

"Yes!" I called back.

"Hail!" shouted Alan.

Jim, Luke, and Bill had joined me in the yard.

"Hail roars?" I shouted.

"Yep!"

By then the billowing, roaring curtain was at the edge of

town and we retreated into the trailer to watch it from the windows. A few seconds later we were being pelted by hail the size of …the size of…(can I do this without a sports metaphor?) … the size of…jawbreakers! The ten-cent ones, not the twenty-five-cent ones.

Hail roars. Who knew? The hailstones bounced noisily off the roofs of our trailers for a few moments and moved on, leaving the yard covered with ice.

Our trailer was rocked by violent storms all night, spoiling everyone's sleep.

One day, while we sat in the trailer waiting for the wheat to ripen, or for "Bonanza" to come on, whichever occurred first, we found ourselves watching Roy Underhill, the primitive carpenter, on PBS. I hadn't seen him in years. I was glad to see he was still alive. I still remember the day he almost cut his thumb off on the air. He didn't even slow down, slinging blood all over his workshop as he wheeled and panted his way through his project, looking at the camera, ignoring the pain, explaining, bending wood to his will.

Today, he was going to show us how to turn a bunch of cedar trees into a bed that anyone would be proud to own, in thirty minutes, using only hand tools from another century. He was still as enthusiastic as he was clumsy, and just as entertaining, as he stumbled and smiled and explained his way through the cedar thicket he'd dragged into his workshop. At the end of Roy's allotted half-hour, the cedar trees were little closer to holding up a mattress than at the start. He had reduced his workshop to a shambles.

Then it was time for "Bonanza: The Lost Episodes." Bill got comfortable with his lemonade-flavored drink in one hand, a bag of microwave popcorn in the other, and a happy gleam of anticipation in his eyes. Jim started a game of solitaire, keeping one eye on the Cartwrights. Luke went to bed for one of his famous marathon naps, "doot dooting" along with the Bonanza theme song as he walked down the hall. I decided to take a walk downtown.

Gettysburg has a small but well-stocked library, I discovered. I went to the checkout counter with *Boots and Saddles* by Elizabeth Custer, and *Bury My Heart At Wounded Knee* by Dee Brown.

The librarian was a tiny old woman with unsteady hands, beautiful delicate skin, and bright blue eyes that looked up at me with a clear, steady gaze through her spectacles. She studied me for a moment.

"Libbie Custer was quite a woman," she said quietly. "And quite a writer, too." She was so old I wouldn't have been surprised if she'd told me she knew Custer's widow personally. She expressed no opinion of Ms. Brown.

There's a street in Gettysburg named Custer Avenue.

We exchanged some small talk and I told her I was especially interested in stories about the town's history.

"Follow me," she said with a smile, and we walked slowly, so slowly, to the back of the library to a room with shelves of books from and about the region. She sat down at a table as I perused the shelves. While I browsed I asked her about Gettysburg, and she told me it was founded by veterans of the Civil War in 1883. Then she went on to tell me about the first woman to settle in Gettysburg; Mary O'Brian. I sat down across the table from her and listened. Her story went something like this:

Mary O'Brian was born Mary Sheehee in 1833 in long-civilized upstate New York. At the age of twenty she married Jeremiah O'Brian. She bore him six children. In 1872 Mary became a widow at the age of thirty-nine.

Then her daughter Amelia passed away. Her daughter Hattie suffered from a lung ailment. Emma, her oldest, moved to Redfield, in Dakota Territory. In 1883, Mary, encouraged by Emma's letters, decided to leave the wooded, well-settled hills of New York where she'd lived all her life.

She shed herself of a lifetime's possessions, packed what little was essential, took a breath, and faced west. She journeyed with her four children by coach, river, and rail clear across the face of her nation, and then out of her nation, out to the territories, out to the wild open plains, so recently wrested from the Sioux.

She had hopes that the clear, dry air would cure Hattie's lungs.

That was the year that a group of veterans had formed a company to develop the town of Gettysburg. Somewhere, probably in Redfield, Mary must have seen an advertisement extolling the golden opportunities for enterprising people in the new town, surrounded by the fertile, virgin prairie earth. After a visit with Emma in Redfield, they proceeded west, over the prairie.

On May 22, 1883, Mrs. O'Brian, her daughters May and

Libbie, her son Charlie, and a fellow traveler—a student minister named Valentine—arrived in wagons at Gettysburg. Hattie had stayed in Redfield with Emma. (I wondered about the young Reverend Valentine. Had he drifted on south and settled by the Niobrara?)

One can only imagine Mary and her companions' reactions when they stopped the horses at the appointed site. Gettysburg was hardly more than an idea. Specifically, Gettysburg was two tents pitched on the open, flat virgin prairie.

Mary stood up in front of the wagon's seat, stretched, and looked around. The low, even horizon curved away from her in every direction. The wind roared past, fluttering her bonnet, urgently smoothing and stroking the lush land, so recently captured, so soon to be tamed.

All was grass. Back to the east, a vague set of tracks meandered a little ways from her wagon and faded out, into the grass.

Small white clouds high in the sky raced their shadows across the grass.

Meadowlarks sang, no doubt. They and their sweet voices dipped and rose on the wind, just above the grass.

The thirsty horses pawed the ground impatiently.

Twelve men, the residents of the two tents, stood looking up at Mary and her daughters with eyes as frank as children's.

Mary's long journey from the wooded, watered, civilized Eastern Seaboard had abruptly ended at a spot in the wild grass not apparently different from any other spot between her and the shy horizon.

Was she daunted? Did she consider, for a moment, telling

the young Reverend Valentine to turn the wagons around and follow their tracks back to Redfield, back to the United States, back to New York, before their tracks faded completely away?

Who wouldn't forgive her if she had done what many others did? We forgive them.

We forgive them their weakness of spirit. We forgive them their caving in to adversity. We forgive them their most un-American activity of turning their backs to the West, and heading back to the sheltering, watery East.

They are turning back still, a century later, back from the parched grass, the played-out soil.

We forgive them all, but we don't remember their names.

Mary O' Brian didn't turn back. She climbed down off the wagon. She and her daughters became the first women residents of Gettysburg, Dakota Territory, population seventeen, including their party of five.

Mary was an enterprising woman. She erected two tents and a rude shack with no floor. She named the shack the Buffalo House Hotel.

As it turns out, Mary was at the vanguard of a flood of immigrants. The town quickly became more than an idea, as families poured in from the east to homestead the land around Gettysburg, and others opened businesses in town.

Mary's hotel was in much demand. By the following spring the Buffalo House Hotel had already evolved into an attractive two-story frame building. It had a nice big porch, a meeting room, a restaurant, comfortable guest rooms, and stables out back.

The Buffalo House became well-known in the territory

for providing warm hospitality and delicious home-cooked meals to weary travelers, whose journeys ended or paused in Gettysburg.

Mary O' Brian became a matriarch to the town. Everyone called her Grandmother. In addition to running the hotel and restaurant with her daughters May and Libbie, she nursed the sick, delivered the babies, and was a true friend to all, whose good judgment could be relied upon. Even though Mary was a Catholic, she graciously allowed both Catholic and Protestant services to be held in her hotel, until a Protestant church was built.

In December, 1884, Mary's daughter Hattie came to Gettysburg. Shortly after she arrived, she caught a bad cold from which she never recovered. After a year of sickness she died on December 4, 1885. Libbie had homesteaded a place southeast of town and they buried Hattie there. They donated the grounds around Hattie's grave to the Catholic Church for a cemetery.

In 1886 a typhoid epidemic struck Gettysburg, which by then had swollen in population to twelve hundred. After nursing others, May was stricken and died on October 6 at the Buffalo House. A month later, Libbie was laid low with the same malady. She died in mid-November. Before she died she willed her claim to her mother.

Four of her six children and her husband had now died before Mary.

South Dakota achieved statehood in 1889.

Mary continued to run the Buffalo House until the spring of 1890, seven short years from the time she'd arrived at

Gettysburg. Then she and her son Charlie moved out to Libbie's farm.

There, on November 17, 1892, Mary O'Brian the widow; founder and proprietress of the Buffalo House; matriarch to a town and a true pioneer; died at the age of fifty-nine. She was buried beside her daughters in the plot she and they had donated to the community for its cemetery.

She lies there still, welcoming weary travelers whose journeys have ended or paused in Gettysburg.

"That's a story from our town for you," the librarian said to me when she'd finished her tale. Her ancient blue eyes sparkled brightly at me across the table. "If you'll excuse me," she said, getting up slowly, "I have to go and read a story to the younger children, now. They'll be here soon." She walked slowly, so slowly away.

I left the library and bought a new pair of cowboy boots. I decided to break them in by taking a walk out to the Catholic Cemetery southeast of town. I walked past a field of rye on the way, under a busy sky. Rain and sun mixed together, clouds rushing east. About the time the cemetery came into view up ahead of me, so did a rainbow, shimmering beautifully in a complete arch from the rye field on my left up over the road and cemetery ahead of me and down again to the earth. I swear I wouldn't make up something that corny.

Mary and her daughter's graves are the most modest ones in the cemetery.

By the time I got back to town, I had a blood blister on my foot from my new boots.

I limped into the barber shop for a haircut. Five old men were sitting in a row. A sixth old man was rising like Lazarus from the chair. The barber, no spring chicken, removed the drape from his customer with a flourish, and a crisp snap. Everyone looked at me. I had the impression that a conversation of many years duration had paused.

The air smelled wonderfully of Lucky Tiger Hair Tonic.

"Help you?" the barber smiled at me.

"I need a haircut," I replied. "Is this the line?"

A gentle wave of mirth rippled down the line of old bellies and chins. "No, no," one gentleman assured me. "We're all just sittin' here a waitin' to die!" More mirth.

"Oh, I see," I said, "so this is that line!"

"Have a seat," said the barber, holding the shroud out in a welcoming, embracing gesture.

While I was in the chair, I asked the barber if he knew where the old Buffalo House Hotel used to be.

"The Buffalo House?" he said with a note of surprise, while he snipped and clipped. "Haven't heard that name in a while. They tore it down in the thirties, I believe. Originally, if I'm not mistaken, it was over there." He pointed out the window and down the street with his comb.

I looked where he pointed, to a conspicuously empty lot in an otherwise full block, right across the street from the Dakota Sunset Museum (which contains not even a whisper about the Buffalo House).

The Buffalo House Hotel was open less than a decade, and has been closed for more than a century, and torn down since the thirties. Its name, however, still resonates like the familiar peal of a church bell through the streets and rooms of Gettysburg, and like a church bell's peal, it grows fainter with each moment.

Harvest crews began to flood into town from all over the plains over the next few days. Crews rolled in from Texas, Kansas, Saskatchewan, Colorado, Missouri, Oklahoma, and other places. The chamber of commerce held a pancake breakfast for us all downtown. Someone said that at harvest time the population of Gettysburg swelled by as much as five hundred. That alone, apart from the value of the wheat we'd bring in, would be quite a boon to a town the size of Gettysburg. Harvest time is good for everyone, and they made us feel welcome.

On Saturday, July 18, we moved all our equipment across the Missouri River to the Cheyenne River Indian Reservation.

We crossed at Whitlock, about fifty miles above Oahe Dam. The east approach to the bridge is sinking away, and it was the site of considerable activity to shore up or relocate the approach. Lake Oahe fills up the river channel in a not unappealing way at the bend at Whitlock. As we pulled off the west end of the bridge, signs informed us that we were entering the Sioux Nation.

The distance from our camp in Gettysburg to the fields across the river is about fifty miles. The country west of the river is uncultivated, and sparsely settled. The land was overrun with Murdo McKenzie's and others' cattle for a short time around the turn of the century. They had leased grazing rights from the Sioux. Cattle are now a rare sight, and the land seems well healed. Antelope, deer, and coyotes abound. We even saw a small herd of well-contained bison.

The terrain is rolling clover land, steeply sloped, and utterly devoid of trees. It was the same rich green, sprayed with yellow, that we'd seen south of Pierre. It looks pretty much the way it must have always looked.

We drove west on U. S. 212 about eight miles, till we got to Reservation Road 8, a good gravel road. We followed 8 southwest about ten miles, roughly paralleling the west bank of the river, though at a considerable distance. We dropped the equipment at a field by the roadside, and Alan cut a sample. It wasn't ready yet. We left the equipment and drove back to Gettysburg.

I wanted to camp out by the fields on the reservation when we began to work them.

On Sunday, Alan, Leota, Bill, and I drove down to Pierre to shop and have lunch. Leota knew of a Wal-Mart there.

Alan entertained Bill and me over lunch by gently teasing Leota. His blood sugar level was high, and Leota, who loves Alan dearly, monitors his diet with relentless vigilance. He sat down at the table with a salad and an empty dessert cup. Leota eyed the dessert cup.

We engaged in quiet conversation as we ate. People sidled past us on their way to and from the salad and dessert bar. Alan managed to accidentally clink his salad fork against his empty dessert cup a couple of times, which stiffened Leota's jaw ever so slightly.

We talked of this and that.

Then, as Alan's salad had diminished to a few scraps of lettuce, he turned to Leota and said, "Leota?"

Leota swallowed, looked pointedly at Alan, and said, "What?"

"Leota, did you see that ice cream over at the dessert bar?" Alan asked, with all the innocence he could muster.

"Forget it," Leota said firmly.

"It won't hurt me."

"No."

"They're small servings. Look!" Alan held up his dessert cup for her to examine. There was a mischievous gleam in his dark blue eyes, opened wide behind his spectacles.

Leota wasn't buying it. "Alan, shut up and eat your salad!" she said firmly. She returned her attention to her own plate.

"Leota?"

"WHAT?"

"The reason I only got salad was so's I could have ice cream."

"When you get down to one-ten, that's fine. Not before." She gave him a stern look.

"Be reasonable. One-twenty."

"One-ten."

There was a pause in the debate as Alan resigned himself to finishing his lettuce, and Leota dug back into her baked potato.

Bill and I munched contentedly on our own more bountiful fare.

"You know," Alan pointed out to us all as he finished his lettuce, "I don't think that's even real ice cream."

"Nusser!" Leota scolded him through clenched teeth, set

down her fork, and raised her hand as if to strike him, much to his amusement.

Monday, we cut wheat. I had packed my tent and some supplies, so when the rest of the crew went back to town at the end of the day, I bade them adieu and pitched my tent on the rim of a hill overlooking a gentle ravine meandering west.

I sat on my sleeping bag in front of my tent and watched the day fade away. The wild clover-covered hills rippled off to the horizon in the waning light, smelling of honey, sensual and pure. Surely the gender of that land is female.

I'd hoped for a raking light as the sun dropped low, but I was disappointed by a low cloud bank that rose up from behind the horizon and captured the sun. Distance in that tree-less, uninhabited country is nearly impossible to estimate, due to the lack of landmarks of identifiable scale. The land itself offers no clue because little hills and big hills all look the same. This is made even more true in a flat light. I don't know how far I could see from my prospect. It seemed like a long way.

Night was a long time coming. In those latitudes in summer the sun rises and sets on such a gradual slope it's like a plane taking off and landing in slow motion.

About 10:30 I took a twilight walk, drinking in the solitude and openness.

When I got back to my tent I made a pot of coffee. I'd brought Sterno, anticipating a lack of fuel. I dug a small, shallow hole in the ground, and punched six holes in the bottom of an empty coffee can. Then I punched six more holes in the sides of the can, near the open top. I set the sterno in the middle of the shallow hole, lit it, and set the coffee can over it, top down. Then I set my coffee pot on the resulting hot surface and waited. Nothing happened so I set the sterno up on a little mound of dirt in the hole to get it closer to the pot. Soon I had a nice, hot cup of coffee.

I sat in front of my tent in the chilling air and sipped slowly from the little vessel of warmth cupped in my hands. Dimness rose up from the earth and gathered in the air.

It never really got dark that night. The twilight went on and on, and then the moon rose, shining its light through a gauze. I dozed off and on, listening to the coyotes.

Just before sunrise I got up and put on another pot of coffee. As I waited for the coffee to perk, it began to sprinkle. I watched a family of deer gamboling across the lawn between me and the combines. The sun began its slow, laborious ascent from way off in the northeast quadrant.

The sprinkles turned to intermittent rain. The Sterno couldn't seem to rouse its' weak flame to the task of boiling water. I waited. I was thick and drowsy from a night of little sleep. The air was chilly and damp. My joints were stiff. I waited and waited for that cheerful gurgle.

Finally, I gathered up some seasoned cow chips, doused them with kerosene from the service rig, and had some by-god coffee.

After coffee, I set out on a hike down the ravine before me, to see what I could see of the lay of the land. The stream in the bottom of the ravine grew as it worked its way down toward the Missouri, which was maybe five or six miles downstream. It intersected with another small stream and the resulting creek formed a small pleasant valley. In the valley I encountered a pack of six coyotes. Their fear of me was checked by their curiosity, so we stayed in each others' vicinities for a long time as I ambled downstream. I would catch glimpses of their ears and noses sticking up over the rim of a rise, and then see them a minute later, scampering over a further hill to wait for me as I followed the creek.

I also saw numerous deer, including two beautiful bucks lying together in a draw in the cool morning air. I got downwind, crawled up close to them, and took their picture. I sat up, focused, and snapped. They stared at me for fully three minutes before they rose and bolted. Maybe I was becoming transparent.

A low, gray cloud mass had pushed in from the west to choke off the weak morning light.

I wandered through a gathering mist back to the tent, and when I got in range, I heard Luke and Jim calling out to me over the service rig's radio. A few minutes later they pulled up in a grain truck. Alan had sent them to unload the grain cart and find out the weather. If they didn't get back to Gettysburg in three hours, Alan and Bill would come ahead ready to cut wheat, for that would mean that Luke and Jim had found dry field conditions.

The weather was threatening, though it wasn't raining at the moment. We headed over to the field and unloaded wheat from the grain cart to the truck, to get the wheat under tarp. Luke and Jim stood around, unable to decide whether to stay or go. It was a little wet, but was it too wet? Would it dry up, or would it rain more? They were hesitant to take responsibility for making the call.

"So," I said at last, "you boys have time to come over to the house for a while?" I nodded at the tent in the distance.

"You got any coffee?" asked Jim.

"Well, I could put on a pot," I replied, with a smile.

We strolled over to the tent. I began to gather up cow chips along the way.

"Uh, what're you a'doin'?" Luke asked me.

"This is for the fire," I replied, my arms full of cowshit.

"Well, ya know," Luke said, "I've never been much of a coffee dranker." That was true.

We spent the next hour working hard to build a fire hot enough to make coffee on that bald, damp plain. Luke got into the spirit, amused by the novelty, and contributed armloads of cowshit to the cause. We doused them with kerosene, set the mess on fire, blew into it, added more, waited for the coffee to perk, and went at it again and again. Finally, we achieved coffee. I poured it, and there was only enough for my guests, much to my chagrin.

The sky began to spit rain.

"Yessir," Luke said, leaning back on one elbow, "I don't usually drank coffee, but I feel like I earned this'n." He surveyed the view to the west. "You picked ye a nice spot," he said, taking a sip.

"Good coffee," said Jim, face buried in a mug.

"You know, boys," I sighed, as I threw another piece of cowshit on the low fire, "It just doesn't get any better than this."

"Most fun I've had all summer," Luke said, without a trace of irony.

It began to rain in earnest. Luke drank his coffee down and Jim, before I could stop him, dumped out what remained in his cup. They offered me a ride back to town.

"No thanks," I said. "I like it here."

They ran through the rain to the service rig, which they were to drive back to town. They had five miles of dirt two-track, including a creek crossing, just to get back to the gravel road, so there was some urgency in their getting out before any more rain fell. In a minute I was alone.

I was about to meet El Niño, face to face.

By mid-afternoon, I'd been trapped in my tent for hours by a hard rain driven by a wild wind which had started out from the south and gradually shifted southeast as it rose in velocity.

The wild wind doesn't howl on the open plains. The wild wind howls when it's trapped, or forced by obstructions to change its direction. The wild wind roars uninhibitedly on the open plains, and it roared around me and my flimsy little dome, my bubble on the grass, with increasing ferocity all day.

The rain steadily, inexorably invaded my tent, pushed by the wind through the flimsy fabric.

I tried to wait out the storm by napping. I figured that it would play itself out after a few hours and settle down. Then I could make some coffee and take a walk along the rushing rivulets.

The assault on my tent only increased as the afternoon wore on to evening. The wind continued to shift to out of the east. When it reached that cardinal point, it increased dramatically in velocity, pushing wave after wave of heavy rain against my tent, which was trying to turn itself inside out. So far the tent had remained resolutely pinned to the earth, but with the sudden rise in wind speed, the most windward peg began to wiggle worrisomely in the soft, soaked mud. I knew if one peg gave way, they all would. The water inside the tent also was getting to be a problem. I didn't want a wet sleeping bag.

El Niño leaned overbearingly on my little tent. The tent's arched poles bent inwards, against me. I crouched in the center, in the green semi-darkness, wrapped in my sleeping bag, lost in the roar of El Niño's endless exhale. The rain fly thrummed against my tent like a flushed quail.

Finally, feeling a little panicky, I packed up what I needed, and wanted to keep dry, and abandoned ship. I arose from the low tent entrance to face El Niño. I leaned forward, my head bowed.

The 150-yard trudge to the tractor was a long, arduous, gloomy swim. I slogged into the wind-driven rain, through gumbo past my ankles, with a loaded duffel bag over my shoulder, one slow step at a time. When I reached plowed ground, the bottom of the earth gave out beneath me, and the last dozen yards or so were a real struggle.

Upon reaching the tractor, I threw myself into the cab and resigned myself to a difficult night.

I was drenched, and freezing cold (in July!), so I turned on the engine, and cranked up the heater all the way. I turned on the radio for weather information and company while I waited for the heater to warm up. It never did. I don't know why.

After shivering in my sleeping bag for a few minutes, I packed up again and headed back out into the mud, wind, and rain over to Jim's combine. The wind pushed the door shut behind me.

A few minutes later I was warm, if not dry. Outside the cab windows the roaring night collapsed down around me.

I didn't sleep that night. I spent the night finding different ways to wrap myself around the steering wheel. Every few minutes I'd turn the engine on to warm back up. Outside the rain just kept coming. It was like sitting in a car wash all night.

As the night wore on the wind continued to shift until eventually it was out of the north-northeast. As it moved away from easterly, it abated somewhat.

I looked across the 150 yards to my tent. One peg had come loose right after I'd abandoned it, but the others clung tenaciously to the mud. The loose, billowing tent writhed and pulled, straining to free itself from the earth.

During the night I began to realize how isolated I was. It would be several days before the boys could get that far back in to retrieve me.

About a quarter to four, dawn became perceptible, even through the cloud cover. By sunrise, the rain had stopped, although the wind hadn't.

Suddenly my tent blew away over the hill it had been perched on.

I stepped outside on the deck of the combine, in the buffeting wind. The wind dragged wave after wave of low, ragged clouds with it, coming endlessly out of the northeast.

I could sure use a cup of coffee, I thought. But of course there wasn't a dry cow chip on that whole reservation, and I wasn't sure I'd ever see my coffee pot again anyway.

I retrieved my tent and carried it back to the combines and hung it on a barbed wire fence to dry. I had to decide what to do with myself. I considered walking out to the river crossing at Whitlock, about twenty-five miles away.

Under better circumstances, I would have welcomed the prospect of such a walk through such perfect walking country. However, I was exhausted after forty-eight hours with little sleep. Also, the weather was cold, the wind was stiff, the mud was deep and slick, the streams were swollen, and the dark clouds were pregnant with the threat of more rain. My other option was to hike three miles further in to a ranch house I'd seen, take my chances on someone being home, and depend on their hospitality until the boys could get in to get me. That would be days, due to the inevitably washed out two-track that led to the gravel road, which may itself have been washed out for all I knew. I couldn't decide, so I stood there in my sleeping bag and did nothing but shiver for a long time.

Suddenly I saw a small vehicle weaving toward me through the grass from the direction of the ranch house. I smiled. I knew that my decision had been made for me.

The vehicle was a Honda four-wheeler. Its driver was a Sioux woman. She pulled to a stop in front of me. Her dog had ridden with her on the back. We exchanged "howdys."

She looked me over and said, "The people you work for called me this morning and said if you wanted out they'd meet you at the gravel road. They're gonna call back. I can give you a ride. Climb on." Her dog sniffed me. I was pretty ripe, no doubt.

I climbed on the back and off we went, plowing through the mud and standing water. I caught all the muck sprayed up by the tires. We flushed up grouse and jackrabbits, to which her dog, now running along beside us, gave spirited chase. We drove past a prairie dog town, where I saw an owl sitting patiently by a hole, waiting.

We pulled up outside the ranch house, which was a mobile home. Here we dismounted, and removed our boots. I was completely covered in mud, so her son and daughter looked me over with wide-eyed amazement when I walked into their living room behind their mother.

"Do you want a cup of coffee?" the woman asked, heading for the kitchen.

My heart leaped! "I can't tell you how grateful I'd be for a cup of coffee," I replied immediately.

She was unable to suppress a smile at the earnestness of my reply. "The bathroom's down the hall if you want to wash up," she suggested.

I thanked her and walked down the hall in my stocking feet. What I saw in her mirror shocked me. I washed until my face emerged from a hole in the mud, cleaning my hands in the process.

"Do you want a shower?" she called to me. She didn't even

know my name. I politely declined. I still had a long, muddy ride ahead of me, which would have rendered it pointless.

Back in the kitchen, I sat down gratefully to a cup of hot coffee. "Thank you," I murmured into the cup.

"Oh, you're welcome," the woman smiled. Her children stared at me.

"My name's Richard, by the way," I said.

"I'm Mary Kay," she replied. "If I'da known you were out there last night I would have come and got you then. I just didn't know."

Her three-year-old son slipped up to me and studied me intently.

"You're sittin' in my daddy's chair," he informed me with a friendly little smile.

"Oh, really?" was all I could think of to say.

The boy's big sister had begun to stare intently at the TV.

"Kenny, that's my husband, got stuck down in Pierre yesterday," Mary Kay informed me. "I almost didn't get in from Eagle Butte, myself, because of the storm."

We made small talk while we waited for the phone to ring. Before long it did. It was agreed that Mary Kay would drive me the eight miles to the gravel road on her Honda four-wheeler. Alan and Bill would meet me there, and take me back to Gettysburg.

"They'll meet us in about an hour," Mary Kay informed me when she got off the phone.

I wondered for a moment if there'd be time for another cup of coffee. Then, realizing how far we had to go, and the conditions, I pushed my cup away and said, "I'm ready whenever you are."

We proceeded forthwith. I climbed on behind her and grabbed hold, and off we went. It was a tight fit, the two of us on that Honda seat, and a rough ride.

Before we'd gone too far I found myself calculating how long I'd been away from my home and wife. I'd been gone from home sixty-eight days and I felt every one of them as we bumped and ground our way the eight miles out to the gravel road. It was an unforgettable journey. By the time we reached the road, after nearly an hour's ride, I was fully awake, alert, and thinking of my wife, so far away.

Alan and Bill pulled up just as we did. I could see them grinning from a hundred yards. I must have been a sight, climbing off the back of that Honda, after eight miles of thick mud and water.

I thanked Mary Kay profusely, for everything. "You're my hero!" I said.

"Glad to do it," she smiled, and drove off.

I offered to ride in the back of the pickup, but Alan insisted I ride in the front. It was beginning to rain again, he pointed out. I peeled off my mud-caked jacket, threw it into the back, and climbed in beside Bill.

On the way back to town, I recounted my adventure and Alan and Bill laughed and laughed. I'd never seen Alan so amused.

The transient, wispy relationships

of people whose bodies had

accelerated along the same paths for a while,

ended as they

oned off on separating trajectories...

Heading South

A few hours later I'd had a long, hot shower, a shave, clean clothes, a hot meal, and a couple of cups of coffee. I was sitting in the trailer with the guys, warm and dry, watching "Mothra," a Japanese science fiction movie.

I became depressed. Incredibly, I wished I was back out there. Something real had happened to me. Out there, out there.

I went to bed early.

The next morning I woke up knowing that I was through. I wanted to go home.

I called the diner and J. J., the dishwasher, answered the phone.

"Hey, Rich!" he said. "How's the search for your destiny goin'?"

"Let me speak to Debbie."

I told Debbie that I'd decided to head south. I just had to wait for the right time.

We had a few days of good weather.

Kenny, Mary Kay's husband, helped us repair the washed-out road to his house and our customer's fields, and then hired us to cut his wheat, too.

After we'd finished up across the river, we turned our

attention to the fields around Gettysburg. We got in several good days of work, though El Niño hovered around always in the corners of the sky.

As for me, my heart was no longer in it. I was just marking time. Meeting El Niño face to face had blown my spirit out and allowed the dark mood of that summer's skies to seep into me. I always felt a little chilly, a little damp, a little dark.

During this period, we began to see a lot of Harley riders roll through Gettysburg. Their annual soiree at Sturgis, in the Black Hills, was starting up.

I heard on the radio that the local hospital in Sturgis was stocking up on blood. The Sturgis police force was broadcasting an appeal for fools to deputize for the weekend.

I overheard two local gentlemen talking about it at the post office as a Harley roared by.

"Stay away from the Black Hills this weekend," said one.

"It'll be plenty dangerous," agreed the other.

"Say, do you know how much the average Harley owner makes a year?" asked the first. "Over thirty thousand. Saw it in the paper."

"Over thirty thousand! That's a lot of money," replied the other. "Must be a bunch of lawyers."

"A hundred thousand drunken lawyers on Harleys," mused the first.

"Like you said," said the other, "stay away from the Black Hills this weekend."

The weatherman predicted rain. I decided if he was right, I'd tell Alan I was through.

The next morning I awoke to the sound of rain on the trailer roof.

Alan came over and offered to take us all out to breakfast. As we settled into the cab of the pickup, I said "Alan, would it screw you up if I packed it in and headed back south from here?"

"No, not really," he replied. He seemed surprised, though not unpleasantly.

"Well, I guess I'll head out, then," I nodded.

We went on to breakfast and nothing more was spoken about it.

When we got back to camp, I packed and a few minutes later Alan paid me off, shook my hand, and we wished each other luck.

Bill drove me down to Pierre. Luke and Jim came along for the ride. They dropped me off at the bus station and drove off after a round of hearty good-byes.

I called Debbie and she offered to drive from Tulsa to Omaha and meet me at the bus station at 2:00 a.m., and take me home. What a woman.

Among the passengers on the bus to Omaha was a forlorn Harley rider in full regalia. He'd wrecked his bike and was heading home to Milwaukee. He didn't look like a lawyer.

Also among the passengers were several men like me who'd cut out from other crews. We passed the time with small talk. Apparently, we decided, South Dakota was where people started peeling off and heading home.

The Omaha bus station in the wee hours of the night is a busy place. People in knots and lines milling and surging between the hissing buses and station doors. People, recently asleep, blinking in the bright lobby lights. People searching for lovers, friends, family, luggage. People in interweaving clusters, some stopping to embrace each other, some shouldering past each other with tired hunter's eyes.

The transient, wispy relationships of people whose bodies had accelerated along the same paths for a while, ended as they now caromed off on separating trajectories, sometimes with a smile or a little wave, a wish of good luck.

Lifelong relationships were reaffirmed as people embraced, searching each others' faces for familiar lines, new scars.

The hissing buses and station doors, the hubbub, the chattering voices, the uncomprehending cries of babies.

Perfumes, cigarettes, diesel, coffee.

The chink and rustle of money changing hands. The clutched tickets.

For a moment I didn't recognize Debbie, moving through the crowd in clothes I hadn't seen before, wearing an expression I also hadn't seen, that of a stranger in a strange land, late at night. A woman looking for her husband. Her hair was longer.

We had a joyful reunion.

As I climbed into the van, a weimaraner pup—the spitting image of Max—gave me a good sniffing.

"His name is Moses," Debbie said. She gave Moses a pat on the head. We found a motel and sneaked Moses inside in a hand bag.

Within twenty-four hours we were back in Tulsa.

Jared, Jennifer, and I mauled each other on sight. Jared had

How Mama Bakes Bread

Four-thirty in the morning, in the diner's kitchen:

"Bread," Mama says, as she dips her greased hands into the steel bowl of risen dough, "is a living, growing thing. You have to understand that if you want to bake."

I want to bake.

"Some people just can't bake, and that's why—they don't think it's alive. They may know it, but they still don't think it, if you get my meaning."

I believe I do.

She pulls out a warm, fleshy wad of dough, feels the weight, and adjusts the amount until it feels right. "Yeast is alive,—we nourish it with sugar and shelter it with warm water to make it grow." She works it around in her hands, stretching it, smoothing and shaping it to fit the bread pan. When it's right she slaps it into the pan and goes on to the next one. She makes about thirty loaves on weekdays, more on the weekends.

"A good baker has an affection for the bread. Wanna try one?"

I want to try one.

I grease my hands and plunge them into the dough. It's soft, springy, and internally warm. It feels alive in the most mammalian way.

"Feel its weight," Mama says. I hold it in one hand, hefting it, absorbing its warmth. "That's how you know you have the right amount for a loaf —by weight."

It seems to grow in volume even as I smooth it, stretch it, and shape it for the bread pan. I lay it gently, affectionately in the pan, like a newborn baby.

I want to do another.

"Tomorrow," Mama says, shouldering me out of the way. "Today, you make gravy."

While I make gravy, she finishes the bread and makes another batch.

She starts with about two quarts of hot water, which she pours into the mixer bowl. This is a pretty big mixer. The steel bowl will hold about three gallons.

She adds ten eggs. "Eggs keep it fresh," she says.

She dips one of those stainless steel cups they use to mix milkshakes into a barrel of sugar and fills it "almost full, but not quite," and adds the sugar to the mix.

She cups her hand and pours salt into it, "just until it starts to run over," and drops the salt in.

She adds two dippers of oil. It looks like about a half-cup dipper.

"Hand me that little blue gravy cup," she says to me, pointing. "The squared off one." She fills it to "just a teeny bit over level full" with yeast, and drops the yeast into the mix.

She takes a potato masher and stirs everything around a little, breaking up the eggs.

"Now the flour." She has a scoop she made by cutting part of the top, including the handle, out of a five-gallon plastic cooking oil container.

"Two scoops —that's heaping scoops—of whole wheat

first, and then five scoops of white. Mix it in with the potato masher until it's where the mixer paddle won't sling loose flour around the kitchen."

When the dough is sufficiently prepared with the potato masher, she attaches the mixer paddle and turns the mixer on. As the mixer kneads the dough, she stands over the bowl with a scoop of white flour, and adds small amounts until the dough has the consistency she's looking for.

She turns off the mixer. "You want it to be firmed up, but still glistening," she says, giving the dough an affectionate pat. "Now we wait for it to rise."

In a few minutes, the dough has grown up over the top of the bowl.

Once she's set the dough into the bread pans, she sets them on top of the pre-heated ovens to rise again in the warmth. This takes a few more minutes. The amount of time the dough takes to rise varies from day to day. She's not always exactly sure why. She thinks humidity is a factor, and of course, room temperature.

When the dough has risen to its full height in the pans, she opens the oven door and, leaning into the escaping heat, she gingerly sets the loaves on the racks, and closes the door.

"How hot do you set the oven?" I asked.

"I don't know the temperature, the thermostat's faulty, but what you do is set the dial exactly horizontal. This oven's touchy. If your dial's off just a hair either way, it throws it way off, so you've got to be really careful."

Thirty to forty-five minutes later, she takes the finished

bread out. It's browned to perfection, and its yeasty aroma fills the room.

We cut off a couple of slices while it's still hot, to check our work, and slather it with margarine. We sit down at a table in the dark, deserted diner, with our bread and coffee.

It is good.

&pilogue

Soon it will be daylight. Through the diner's frosty windows, I see headlights sweep across a road sign out by the street. "Route 66," shaking in the winter wind.

My third cup of coffee sits tepid beside me on the counter. The room is filled with the aroma of bread ready to come out of the oven.

I remember when I used to wonder if I'd been saved or captured by this place. I never really answered that question— I just stopped asking it.

Not long after I got home, I asked Mama to teach me how to bake bread. I met her at the diner at 4:30 every morning to help knead the dough, grease the pans, load the ovens—until she judged that I'd become sensitive enough to the dough to be left alone with it.

It's risen enough to put in the oven, she tells me, when it feels just like a woman's breast.

I've been thinking about this place, lately. I think that when the weather warms up I'd like to give it a fresh coat of paint. Some nice soft shade of yellow ochre about waist high all the way around the building, and above that, cerulean blue all the way up to the eaves. I'll trim the windows all in white.

Debbie and the crew will be here in a few minutes to get the place ready to open for the day. Stamping the cold from their feet, hanging up their coats. Women bearing vessels, stirring the day's first laughter up from a coffee cup. Someone will turn the signs around.

Then the hungry crowd will come jingling through our door, smiling with anticipation, comforted by the pungent, earthy aroma.

I will watch them raise my bread to their lips, lips pausing in conversations, conversations arising all around me, and I'll take my own comfort.

THANK YOU

KATHY AND VERNON HIGGS
for raising me in the country

ELAINE SANDERS
for teaching me how to spell forty

DOROTHY CRAIN (MAMA)
for teaching me the art of baking

ANNA
for lending me your camera

THE DAVIDS: BLUST, PROEBER, AND VARMECKY
OF THE TULSA PHOTOGRAPHY COLLECTIVE
*for teaching me the difference
between "taking" a photograph and "making" one*

LARRY AND NATALIE GREEN OF APERTURES
for taking care of my negatives

PAULETTE, MICHAEL, SALLY, AND CAROL
AT COUNCIL OAK BOOKS

MIKE FLANAGAN
for long-ranging walks and wide-ranging talks

And, of course,

ALAN AND LEOTA NUSSER